Urges

Gary Hennerberg

Urges

Copyright © 2009 by Gary Hennerberg

We want to hear from you. Feedback or requests for information should be directed to gary@hennerberg.com

ISBN 978-144-8690-831

All rights reserved. No part of this publication may be reproduced, stored in a retrieval system, or transmitted in any form or by any means — electronic, mechanical, photocopy, recording, or any other — except for brief quotation in printed reviews, without the prior permission of the author.

Doses of Comfort Publishing

www.Manage-Trich-Urges.com

Book design by Perry Steinhoff

Cover photograph by Perry Steinhoff with assistance from Merri Alexander Bass. He can be reached at perry.steinhoff@gmail.com.

Back cover photograph by Jean Ann Bybee and Brad Rogers. They can be reached at www.bybeephoto.com.

Printed in the United States of America.

About the Cover Photograph

Throughout this book, Gary Hennerberg describes himself as a complex weave of fabric. Within that weave are imperfect threads... some frayed... some with multiple colors... others with multiple textures... some criss-crossed... each symbolizing the intricate wiring of our minds.

The cover photograph of the multi-colored scarf symbolizes the multiple textures and patterns of fabric that Hennerberg uses to describe his life with trichotillomania.

The heart-shaped box is a reminder of the need for unconditional love for children and adults with trichotillomania or any other compulsive disorder. The photo on the tabletop is of Hennerberg as a 9-year-old.

Praise for Urges

"Gary Hennerberg provides a vivid account of the sensations and emotions of growing up with trichotillomania, the compulsion to pull out his own hair. His story is interwoven with richly detailed anecdotes of childhood on a family farm at the Nebraska and Kansas border in the 1960s.

"Hennerberg grew up with strong faith and loving parents during a seemingly 'simpler time' in the American heartland, but life wasn't so simple for a complex boy with a complicated problem. The urge to pull out his hair was a closely kept secret for most of Hennerberg's life and he describes how it impacted his development. The book also gives insight into his parents' struggle to understand and help their child in an era when no one had heard of this disorder and no information or treatment was available.

"Ultimately, Hennerberg's memoir is a journey to self-acceptance. His Christian faith is an integral part of his experience and is expressed primarily in his advocacy of unconditional love. Readers will be heartened to learn that despite his struggles, the author has achieved a happy life with a strong marriage, children, and friendships."

Jennifer Raikes
Executive Director
Trichotillomania Learning Center (TLC)

"Many books have been written about trichotillomania from doctors, therapists and sufferers. This book defines trichotillomania from a man's journey through childhood to the present. Gary offers hope through his journey of spiritual healing. Young boys with trichotillomania have been largely ignored. Now they have a role model. This is a *must* read for anyone dealing with this devastating disorder."

Joan Kaylor, MSEd, LPC
Former hair puller, past TLC board member,
and trichotillomania counselor

"I have trichotillomania ... I never thought that there would be others out there suffering as well. I was blessed to read Gary's book and this book is truly incredible! His perseverance is astonishing, and it helped inspire me to talk to my Teen Leadership class about my struggle with trichotillomania. I read my class an excerpt from a chapter in this book, and they all thought it was amazing. *Urges* is one big emotional roller coaster, and I loved every second of it!"

Stephen, a 16-year-old hair puller

"This is a book on a subject something no one talks about. It is also a book about the power of faith, hope, and prayer to transform even our most hidden issues into resurrection moments. As Gary shares his story and his struggle, he allows us to enter into the painful world of those who suffer from compulsive disorders. This book is about hope and the healing that can occur through bringing our darkest secrets into the light."

Dr. Cindy Ryan
Pastor and Author

Gary Hennerberg
In 1965 at the age of 9
when much of his hair had been pulled out.

Dedications

To my Dad and Mom,

> For your unconditional love and parenting when we thought I was the only child in the world who pulled my hair

To my wife, LoCinda,

> For your love and acceptance of me as I am, without ever judging or rejecting me for having this unexplainable disorder

To my daughters, Amy and Liza,

> For being the most wonderful daughters a father could ever hope to have raised ... I can't imagine life without you

And to hair pullers and those with other compulsive disorders,

> It is my hope that you find self-acceptance and learn to co-exist with trichotillomania or whatever mysterious urges consume you

Table of Contents

Foreword from Christina Pearson	xiii
1. Defining Moment	1
2. Grace	11
3. Dreams	21
4. Blessings	29
5. Sequencing	37
6. Wiring	43
7. Shame	49
8. Compassion	55
9. Church	63
10. Strength	71
11. Unconditional Love	81
12. Looping	93
13. Perfection	101

14. Grooming	113
15. Horns	123
16. Amputation	131
17. Blame	137
18. Trust God	153
19. Hair Replacement	161
20. Love of Life	179
21. Generations	187
22. Reinventing Myself	195
23. Turning Point	209
24. Afterword	219
25. Prayer	221

FOREWORD
By Christina Pearson
Founding Director
Trichotillomania Learning Center

Slowly, a voice is rising. This voice is one of a disorder that has been around perhaps forever (as far as humans are concerned), but never acknowledged, listened to, or given solace. It is the voice of trichotillomania (TTM, "trich"), or compulsive hair pulling.

So much suffering has been endured by those struggling with this problem, and yet few even knew it existed. Until now.

Finally, as a result of tireless hard work and perseverance, the medical, research, and therapeutic communities are beginning to take seriously the distressing challenges of hair pulling and related disorders such as skin picking.

Along with many others, I have devoted the past two decades to raising public awareness, developing resources, and consulting with clinicians to improve treatment. Through these efforts a wonderful national organization has evolved to serve the trich community — the Trichotillomania Learning Center (TLC). TLC is very much a grassroots organization, primarily funded by sufferers and their family members through memberships, donations and attendance at our events. It has been a

Urges by Gary Hennerberg

slow and difficult road, but I do believe that we are finally at the tipping point, and that things will move more quickly from now on in this field. A clear indicator of this is that more and more people in the general public are vaguely familiar with trich, and the word itself has been the winning clincher in at least one spelling bee!

TLC is working to support rigorous scientific research, developing training materials for treatment providers, and constantly adding to our resources, all to better serve the community. Concurrently to these efforts, more and more individuals like Gary Hennerberg are stepping up to share their personal experiences with this misunderstood and often misdiagnosed disorder. Ultimately, this will help others come to terms with their own struggles in healthier ways, and lay the groundwork for what I hope will be a public awareness paradigm shift. The landscape for those of us who struggle with this problem is finally changing! There is still a long way to go, but today the road is becoming both easier to navigate - and - there are more folks willing to walk openly upon it.

Gary's personal story, his intimate sharing of the progression of the disorder and its impact on his life, is a poignant one. A classic tale of a Midwestern farm upbringing, both his struggles and the perseverance to succeed in spite of the trich come through loud and clear.

Foreword

There are still very few personal memoirs about this subject, and up until now I believe not any from a man's perspective. That makes this book even more valuable, as I hope it opens the door for other men to step forward, release feelings of isolation and shame, and seek relief.

It is only when we are willing to own the truth of our experience that we can then take the necessary steps to change our world, and thus also impact the world of those around us.

Gary has owned his truth, and given voice to his experience. May his insights and evident loving nature provide a source of inspiration and motivation to all who read this book!

Christina Pearson
Founding Director
Trichotillomania Learning Center
www.trich.org

CHAPTER 1
Defining Moment

I'm a hair puller. I've lived with this mysterious urge since the age of six.

I enjoy it. I get a rush from doing it. It's euphoric.

I hardly realize when I'm doing it. It happens when my mind has gone on autopilot or when I'm reading, watching television, or bored. I'm in a virtual trance.

It begins with movement of my left arm and hand toward my head. I'm right handed, but my right hand isn't the perpetrator. It's the left hand that's the bad boy.

I feel for textures. I like to touch the raw scalp from where I've most recently pulled. The skin is so soft. So innocent. No stubs. So smooth. It's perfect. And as I touch the hair surrounding where I've previously pulled, I start to twirl hair. I'm searching for the perfect hair to pull. Maybe it's extra curly. Or coarse.

Sometimes I twirl a few strands of hair. The twirling action knots the ends of the hair together. Ah, I have a small bunch. And I twirl and twirl, maybe ten seconds.

Then I tug them, but don't pull them out just yet. My heart races with anticipation. I tug again. Then I suddenly

Urges by Gary Hennerberg

yank them out. I can hear it! There is no other sound to describe it. The sensation is exhilarating! It stings yet I feel a cool sensation from air touching my raw scalp. It's exposed! To air! To light!

But the prize is between my index finger and thumb of my left hand. I look between my finger and thumb and there it is: the newly pulled hair.

There's more to my hair pulling ritual. I gaze at it. Almost lovingly. I look at the root. White. With a dark spot at the end where the hair was closest to my brain. The root has a sticky substance on it and it clings to my finger.

Sometimes I strip the root from the hair. Sometimes I press the root to my lips, but I don't ever put the hair in my mouth.

Then, with the hair having served its purpose, I drop it. As my spent hair cascades to the floor, my euphoria crashes to earth.

But I can't stop now! Not yet! I have to keep going. I have to recharge the exhilaration. So I continue pulling to lift my spirits, revive my euphoric feeling, and silently bring me joy. I must pull again and again, repeating the twisting of my hair, tugging it, pulling it, looking at the root and dropping it to the floor. Am I crazy? Who in their right mind does this and thinks that this is a good idea?

But at some point I have to stop. And when I look at the dozens and sometimes hundreds of strands of hair on

1 — Defining Moment

the floor, I can't believe my eyes. I've gone from euphoria to emotional devastation in seconds. I don't understand why this is happening to me.

Over the years I've asked myself every question imaginable.

Why do I pull my hair?

Why did God instill in me this urge?

Why didn't God answer my prayers when I cried out for help?

Was God listening?

Were my prayers ignored? Or were they not loud enough to get God's attention?

Or are there two of "us" inside my mind attempting to win control over who I am?

There have always been more questions than answers. But today I know that my hair pulling urge has a name: trichotillomania. What a word. It makes me sound crazy. I'm not. I'm actually quite normal. I thought I was the only person on this planet who had urges to pull my hair for most of my

> I thought I was the only person on this planet who had urges to pull my hair. Now I know that perhaps 10 million other people in the U.S. have hidden their hair pulling urges and have suffered in silence. ~

life. It turns out I'm not alone. Now I know that perhaps 10 million other people in the U.S. have hidden their hair pulling urges and have suffered in silence. This disorder is sometimes thought of as an obsessive compulsive disorder, although trichotillomania isn't scientifically defined as OCD.

"Trich" (pronounced "trick") is a highly focused repetitive action that after a lifetime of hair pulling has become deeply grooved into my psyche. It's a part of me that's deeply woven into the fabric of who I am. And it will never go away.

It was after noon the day it first happened. I remember it like it was yesterday. A warm fall day in 1962 — probably in October, and probably about the time of my sixth birthday when I was in the 1st Grade. It was harvest season on the farm. That time of year when Dad would bring out the combine to harvest the crops. When it was harvest season, there was urgency in the air because the crops were ready and the weather could turn any day, making it difficult to bring in the fall harvest — the paycheck that we had waited for so long to be able to collect.

We had a 1951 GMC pick-up truck. We called it Jimmy. We also called it the Red Horse because it had been used many times in the pasture to help round up cattle.

1 — Defining Moment

During harvest, neighbors helped each other if they could. A neighbor named Bill, who was nearing retirement, was helping Dad that day. I don't know what he was doing, or why he was driving Jimmy, but I do remember that he invited me to ride along to the field to watch Dad combine milo, a crop grown to feed to livestock.

I climbed in the back of the truck. There were boards on the side and across the top so it was completely enclosed. The back of the truck had been cleaned out, so perhaps I rode there for the novelty of being in back and completely surrounded by the boards. I couldn't possibly get out. There must have been a fascination with riding in the back. Who knows? I was only about six, doing illogical things that small children do.

Bill drove into the milo field that had just been harvested. The field was rough. There were ruts in the earth from rainfall during the spring and summer after the crops had been planted. Jimmy didn't have shocks, or if it did, they were completely worn out.

The field was bumpy. But as we drove through it, one rut was apparently deeper than most and as we hit it I was thrown and hit my head on the boards above. It wasn't enough to knock me out. But it was enough to cause a welt to appear on my head, on my left side, above my ear.

Urges by Gary Hennerberg

It hurt. But a few days later, I discovered that gently touching it gave me a sense of peace. It felt good to feel it. Soothing. Calming.

Touching the welt was so peaceful, so serene, that for motivations and reasons I'll never know, I suddenly pulled a hair. Maybe I was experimenting just to see how it would feel. Maybe it was accidental. It doesn't matter. Pulling that hair felt good. It gave me a tingling rush.

Pulling that hair was soothing to the welt and it gave me an emotional lift. It felt so good that I pulled another hair. And another. And I continued pulling. I don't know how long I pulled, but time became meaningless as I pulled my hair.

In just a few minutes I had pulled enough hair to leave a circular shaped bald spot about the size of a dime. It was on the left side of my head, above my ear. The welt was exposed. The skin was smooth to the touch of my fingertips and I was fascinated with the sensation.

I couldn't see the damage until I was back in the house and looked in a mirror. I was stunned to see what I had done. I

> That day was the start of a lifetime of emotional turmoil, zigzagging from the highs of hair pulling euphoria to the depths of devastation for what I had done.

1 — Defining Moment

had to hide it so I combed my hair over the bald spot. Even though I was only six, I knew that pulling hair wasn't natural. That day was the start of a lifetime of emotional turmoil, zigzagging from the highs of hair pulling euphoria to the depths of devastation for what I had done. It would be a day that I wish I could take back and have never experienced — a day that would forever alter the fabric of my soul.

That fall day was a defining moment in my life. How I wish it could have been taken back and started anew.

What if Bill hadn't asked me to ride along to the field that day to see my Dad?

What if I hadn't been adventurous and sat in front of the pick-up instead of in the back?

What if Bill hadn't hit that rut? And if I hadn't hit my head?

What if I just wouldn't have put my fingers on my head and yanked out a hair?

Why did God allow this to happen? I didn't ask for a life of torment and shame from pulling my hair that would consume me. Why didn't God answer my prayers? Jesus healed the sick and performed miracles. I need a miracle! Did the devil step in instead and guide me along?

Urges by Gary Hennerberg

I could blame the series of events from that fall day in 1962 for a lifetime of anguish. It's so easy to rerun an incident over and over again in our minds with the "what if" question.

But I now accept and believe that I was destined to pull my hair. If it hadn't been the incident of the whack on my head and the welt that appeared, it would have been something else. It just would have been another day. With a different trigger.

Research tells me the thump on my head didn't cause it. There are so many other people like me who pull hair. Other hair pullers have been interviewed on ABC's 20/20 where trich has been called a medical mystery. Trich has also been featured on the A&E television show Obsessed. *There is indeed something different about the composition of the brain of a person with trichotillomania.*

But I didn't know that as a child. I believed I was the only person in the entire world who pulled my hair. While it's relieving to know there could be as many of 10 million of us in the U.S. — and an unknown number worldwide — who pull hair, that fact doesn't change the emotional havoc of dealing with trichotillomania.

> I'm determined to co-exist with trich and accept it as part of how God created me.

My life has been molded by trich. But I refuse to let it consume me in a negative way. I'm determined to co-exist with trich and accept it as part of how God created me. It's in my DNA. I'm determined to shift from being a victim to discovering how it has shaped me into the human being that I am today.

Chapter 2
Grace

I believe that God created us to be human and imperfect. My faith and belief in the grace of a higher power has given me peace to accept the complex fabric of who I am.

I didn't come into this world wanting to pull my hair. I've fought it for my entire life. Resisted the urges. Yet caved in time after time.

"Why, God, did you do this to me?" I've prayed many times. I've never heard a definitive answer for "why," but the reason has become more evident to me as the years pass.

Early in my life when I was perhaps 4 years old, a couple of years before I started to pull my hair, a few words from my Mother instilled within me a spiritual insight into "why" it's okay for me to be who I am and accept myself for who I am. At the time she said these words, she could never have had a clue to know that I'd carry this memory with me forever. It's a *reminder to be thoughtful about what we say to our children, for words have the capacity to change a soul.*

The words she spoke came because of a question I asked her after a tragic incident involving the child of neighbors who lived on a farm nearby. This young teen died in a farm accident. I didn't know him, he was around 14 I'd guess, and I was only about 4 years old.

But this boy's sudden death, how his Mother went on with her life, and how my Mother explained the death of the neighbor's boy to me have gone on to serve as a foundation for my faith. A few reassuring words from my Mother taught me about spirituality and how to move forward with my life when times are rough.

My first childhood home in south central Nebraska only had three rooms. The plumbing was "out back." Back then, in the late 1950s it was just me, Mom and Dad. Dad was a farmer. Mom was a traditional farm housewife who not only kept the house and prepared our meals, but helped Dad with chores.

The house and barnyard were down a long driveway, perhaps a quarter of a mile, from the gravel road. As you would turn onto the dirt road you would drive past fields on each side for about one hundred feet. Then the land would turn from farmland to pasture before the road reached a bridge taking you over a creek.

2 — Grace

It wasn't much of a creek. It would dry up to nothing but a ditch during the summer when the natural springs would no longer support it. But when it rained, it was a flowing channel of water, sometimes going over the road and isolating our house from the road.

Beyond the creek, the driveway went past a corncrib on the right with a fenced-in yard for cattle. The buildings on the yard consisted of a barn, machine shed, garage, and other smaller storage buildings. Being near a creek, we had large cottonwood trees in the yard, and in the back, apple trees.

We lived in a white two-story home with three rooms on the first floor plus a closed in porch on the south side of the house. You could enter the house from the south side through the porch into the kitchen. Or you could enter from the north side directly into the kitchen. The outhouse was on the north side, only a few steps from the kitchen door. I don't know what was upstairs. I never went up there. Ever.

Another room on the ground floor was a bedroom. And the third room was a family room where there were chairs and couches and a table and lamp. There was wallpaper on the walls. A floral pattern. Reminiscent of the style from the 1950s.

Urges by Gary Hennerberg

We were poor. We were Nebraskans although our home was only a half-mile north of the border with Kansas.

I don't have a lot of memories of that farmstead, since we moved away from it when I was five, but an incident while growing up there remains one of my earliest memories.

I hadn't started pulling my hair yet at this age. But this memory of words told to me by my Mom has given me comfort in my lifetime. Perhaps it's this memory that gave me my foundation of faith in God and Jesus Christ ... a faith that I would draw upon throughout my life.

Mom and Dad were talking with hushed voices. I knew something bad had happened. Even as a small child, you sense when things are good and when they're bad. Mom and Dad were seated at the kitchen table in our three-room farm home. It was evening, with Dad's field work and chores of milking cows over for the day.

The teenage son of neighbors had been killed that day in a tragic tractor accident. We lived only a mile or so from them. They lived on the state line road, the north side, in Nebraska.

The neighbor boy lost control of a tractor in a field. It rolled over and pinned him underneath. Farm accidents happened, probably everyday somewhere a few generations ago. Equipment didn't have the safety devices that they do today. Boys who were too young to judge the balance of equipment, along with rough conditions of the field, could fall victim to the power of a tractor. It was a scene that played out too often, and one that made me fearful of driving a tractor myself someday.

When a young life was lost, everyone grieved. On the farm, with close-knit families and neighbors, it was a custom for the farm wife to bake a pie, or casserole, and take food to the grieving family. My mother was a wonderful cook, and she followed the custom when she baked a pie and delivered it to the neighbors. I rode with her to the neighbor's farm.

"Stay in the car while I take this in," she told me while I sat silently in the front seat of our car. She went in the house and stayed inside only a few minutes before returning. It was a sad day, and no doubt in her mind she thought of me, her young son, who someday would be old enough to drive a tractor, too. Fearful, perhaps, that someday the same tragic fate could take me away from her.

The tradition of baking a pie or cooking food and delivering it to the family who had lost a loved-one had an outcome that also helped the grieving process. It meant the grieving family would bring back the pie plate which would help them reconnect with family and friends.

Urges by Gary Hennerberg

A few days after the funeral, I was playing outside in front of our house. A car that I didn't recognize drove slowly down our long driveway from the East, across the creek bridge, with dust trailing it in the distance.

It was the mother of the boy who had been killed, and my Mom must have intuitively known she was coming, for she met her in the front yard before she could get out of her car.

I'll never forget the glow of happiness on the face of that boy's mother. It was a radiance I hadn't seen before. I was confused. How could she be so happy? Her son had been killed in an accident and she had buried him only days before.

I continued to play while Mom and the neighbor lady talked for a few minutes. She was older than my Mother. My Mother was about 25 at the time. After just a few minutes of chatting, the neighbor lady smiled, said good-bye, and left. As she drove away, I looked at my Mom. She had sat down on the concrete steps outside our front porch, probably still in deep thought from the conversation only moments before. Perhaps she, too, was dealing with grief. I walked over to her, and sat on her lap.

"Why was she so happy?" I asked.

There was a deafening silence for a moment, since I'm sure my young Mother didn't know how to answer my question. But her answer was one that I'll remember forever:

"She's happy because her son has gone to heaven to be with Jesus."

> "She's happy because her son has gone to heaven to be with Jesus."

My faith has been strong all my life, even during the darkest of times. But it would have been easy for me to have given up on God a long time ago.

I used to believe that I was the only person in the world who had the urge to pull my hair. I couldn't talk about it. To anyone. It was a deep dark secret. Oh, I reasoned that God and Jesus had to know that I did it. I prayed to them a lot about it. I kept asking them to make me stop. But they didn't. And I couldn't — some might say wouldn't — stop on my own. Remarkably, I never blamed God. I was, after all, the one falling short. And I was ashamed.

I feared that if anyone found out that I enjoyed pulling my hair I would be ostracized and would be forever labeled a freak. I lived most of my life being secretive while I hid this unexplainable obsession.

But once I reached my 50s, I decided not to hide this disorder any longer. In some respects, I find strength in accepting the urge to pull my hair, for through it, I have discovered other inner talents and strengths. There are dichotomies, too, and I've managed a way for the individual threads of my soul, and the resulting complicated weave of fabric, to live together in harmony.

But for nearly 50 years of my life — all but the first six or so — there was no harmony for me living with the urge to pull my hair. It was struggle. It was painful. It defined me over the years.

I sense that before I was even born that God had predetermined my make-up ... my DNA ... the complex fabric that defines me.

Within that God-given fabric would be gifts. It would be God's challenge for me to discover and share them.

I would have strengths. They were there for me to draw upon when I needed them to overcome weakness and accomplish goals.

There would be weaknesses. We all have them. How I would seek balance between my strengths and weaknesses would be a life's challenge. A delicate balancing act for me to learn how to manage.

This "issue" of hair pulling was how I was created and I would carry it with me for my entire life. It was something I had to co-exist with. It would be my choice how to deal with it and how to integrate and accept it as part of my spirit.

Perhaps I've rationalized that trich is God-given to keep my sanity. And if trich is God-given then I'm not to blame and I don't feel so badly about myself. Maybe. It's a way I've shifted this "blame thing." If this is God-given — God's will — then I accept it with peace.

This journey with compulsive hair pulling — trichotillomania — has encouraged me to grow spiritually. I've been asked how it is that faith won out over anger, questioning and bitterness. I don't have the answer, except that perhaps God's influence in my life is so strong that only faith could, and would, win.

I know today that trich isn't a mental disorder. There is something physically different about my brain. Just as I suspect people with their own issues may be wired differently.

There are so many issues that people deal with in our world. Perhaps it's an eating disorder. Skin picking. Cutting. Gambling. Hoarding things. Compulsively shopping. Becoming addicted to the Internet. Shoplifting. Being mesmerized by fire. Relying on alcohol to get through the day. Preying on children. Or any one of literally dozens, perhaps hundreds of issues. Some that are so private, so dark, so secret, that we may not even know they exist.

> There are so many issues that people deal with in our world. Some that are so private, so dark, so secret, that we may not even know they exist.

Urges by Gary Hennerberg

> *But I'm at peace with having trich. For I have faith that this urge is God-given, a challenge and a struggle that I will live with daily for the rest of my life.*

Chapter 3
Dreams

"And here's Ste-e-e-v-e Hart!"

I could hear that distinctive voice as it introduced me. I would confidently strut from behind the curtain and the audience would applaud and cheer. They were there to hear me. I would talk. I could sing!

Steve Hart was my imaginary name. A stage name. The one I would use someday when I would be famous and on television.

Like every small child, I had dreams. Innocent dreams. The kind of dreams that every 4 or 5 year-old has. Some kids dream of being a sports star. Some want to be a firefighter. Others dream of following their parent's footsteps. My dream was to be on TV.

But not all dreams are realized. For one thing, there are only so many dreams that can reasonably be achieved in a lifetime.

> When I realized that no one would want to watch TV and see someone who pulled his hair and had bald spots — weirdly placed bald spots — my dream had to evaporate.

Urges by Gary Hennerberg

At some point we change a dream to a goal and ultimately a reality. That's a dream come true.

But not all dreams come true. Life happens. We get to a fork in the road and we take one direction, forsaking the possibilities that could have been had we taken another direction at a pivotal time in our lives.

Some dreams aren't realistic. We walk away. Or we take it away from ourselves.

I took away my dream to be on TV when I was a teenager. I knew it could never happen.

When I realized that no one would want to watch TV and see someone who pulled his hair and had bald spots — weirdly placed bald spots — my dream had to evaporate.

I wanted this bizarre urge to pull my hair to go away. I fantasized that when the urge would go away, my hair would grow back and I'd appear normal like most everyone else.

But that wasn't meant to be.

⸺

My mother was only 21 years old when I was born. Back in the 1950s that wasn't so unusual. She and my Dad were married in 1953 when she was just 18 and my Dad was 27. I can only imagine the whispers from a few people because of the age difference.

I was their first child, born in October of 1956, in a hospital on the second floor of a bank building in Fairbury, Nebraska, about 15 miles from the farm where I grew up.

3 — Dreams

It was a Sunday afternoon around 4 o'clock. To this day, my mood is different on Sundays right about 4 o'clock. I don't know why.

We were among the first in rural south central Nebraska to have a black and white television. We could watch just one station, KOLN-TV from Lincoln. Every Sunday night we watched Ed Sullivan, but every day I dreamed of being a TV star.

We didn't really watch a lot of TV. Mainly because there was plenty of work to do on the farm. And probably because back in those days, there really wasn't that much to watch that would hold our attention.

There was a lot to do outside when the weather was nice. Behind our house was a grove of tall cottonwood trees. They soared into the sky probably 60 or 80 feet in height. I would go in the back yard to play. There were also apple trees, but I don't recall that they produced many apples.

There were animals, too. Dad had cows he milked, a few pigs, and chickens. My folks later told me how much I would play with the chickens.

Apparently I loved feeding the chickens with corn from the corncrib. Even though I don't recall the incident, one day I put a kernel of corn in my nose. My parents could see it, but they couldn't get it out. Eventually, they took me to the doctor who finally pushed it through with the hope it would go into my stomach and pass. Apparently it did. Thankfully, I was so young I don't recall this experience.

The chickens, animals, trees behind the house, and other farmyard diversions couldn't stop my imagination of being Steve Hart. He was a part of my childhood fantasy. I don't know if Steve Hart was an actor or singer. Perhaps he was both. Or maybe he was a newscaster, in the mold of Walter Cronkite whom we would watch on the *CBS Evening News*. Steve Hart would have been multi-talented, because my expectations of him were very great.

But it wasn't just my expectations of Steve Hart that were great. Ultimately, my expectations of myself became very high. I became obsessed with perfectionism. Things needed to be clean and in place. There needs to be an order around me and in my life. I count when I take steps. I get stuck with a thought and roll it over again and again in my mind and wishing I could change it. I repeatedly check to make sure I have locked a car door or closed a garage door. If the thought is introduced in my mind that I may have failed to lock a door, I become concerned

> As a child, I would swell with pride when someone noticed that I looked nice.

that someone will break into my home or car. I know this is irrational. But it's a trait that people with compulsive disorders exhibit.

I've always been a stickler for appearing clean and neat. As a child, I was tall and chubby. I was always bigger than most kids my age, and as an adult I'm taller than most people around me.

My chubbiness as a child bothered me. I tended to move more slowly than other kids. Even though I might have been good at a sport like basketball because of my height, I wasn't interested in team sports.

I was a loner, an unexplainable juxtaposition with my desire to become Steve Hart, the famous guy you'd see on TV. But as I've discovered, even loners can feel comfortable in front of an audience.

For me, it was always important that I looked good. I wanted my clothes to be clean and pressed, as well as fashionable, up-to-date, colorful and eye-catching. But I didn't have clothes like that. My Dad worked hard as a farmer, but there wasn't much extra money for clothes. As a child, I would swell with pride when someone noticed that I looked nice. It's the kind of compliment I still love to receive. There was even a time when I wanted glasses because I thought they would make me look more sophisticated. Later in my adult life, I read a book about love languages and learned that words of affirmation are important to me.

I know that our lives are a fabric woven by events and circumstances of the years preceding the present. My obsessions with being clean were thwarted by life on the farm and a lack of having inside plumbing and having enough water for daily baths. I didn't like being dirty. My desire to have nice clothes couldn't happen. And my dream to be on television couldn't be fulfilled when later the effect of my hair pulling obsessions would permanently change my appearance — one of the most important parts of my fabric — and I would be scarred for life by my own doing.

> My dream to be on television couldn't be fulfilled when later the effect of my hair pulling obsessions would permanently change my appearance — one of the most important parts of my fabric — and I would be scarred for life by my own doing.

As I look back at whom I wanted to be and what I wanted to do — my dream to be on TV — I now realize that

I've achieved much more than I could ever have dreamed back then.

I've overcome odds that I have placed in front of myself. While I would never become the television star of my dreams, I would later discover my ease with being in front of an audience. That skill would serve me well in my life. While I would never become a professional singer, I've been able to discover a place to channel my love of singing and music.

I found love along the way, too, both with my soul mate and my daughters.

> I have learned acceptance of myself, and realize that my compulsive urge to pull my hair may be more of a blessing than a curse.

Importantly, I have learned acceptance of myself, and realize that my compulsive urge to pull my hair may be more of a blessing than a curse.

Chapter 4
Blessings

It's a vivid recollection. Not really a memory. Something that I know deep down happened.

The messenger isn't clear. Perhaps she was an angel. The message was delivered so softly and gently. Nothing brash. It was encouragement and reassurance all in one.

The message was that I would be placed on earth with a multi-faceted personality. A complicated weave in the fabric of my soul.

And that among my many traits, I would pull my hair.

It was God's gift to me. A blessing. Oh, I wouldn't see it that way for a long time. But I would be blessed with a particularly loving mother and a father who would only want the very best for me.

> I believe I was in my mother's womb when this message was delivered to me.

At first I thought I received the message while on another planet. Or perhaps suspended in space somewhere in heaven. But now I believe I was in my mother's womb when this message was delivered to me.

Urges by Gary Hennerberg

In March of 1961, when I was four, we moved away from the Nebraska farmstead. The new place was only about four miles away, but it was across the state line in Kansas. The house was big and beautiful. Two stories, a bedroom for me, and another for my sister who had been born just a few months earlier. Notably, there was an inside bathroom. The exterior was brick. It was a mansion compared to what we had moved from.

Moving across the state line also put us closer to a different town, named Hollenberg. So we were the Hennerberg's from Hollenberg.

Our farm was about a half mile or so north of town. It wasn't much of a town. Maybe 50 people back in the early 1960s. I can vaguely recall the time when there were two grocery stores, probably about the size of a couple of rooms in a house, a lumber store, post office, elevator, blacksmith, even a creamery. All that's mostly gone now.

There was also a school for grades 1 through 12. There wasn't a kindergarten class back in those days.

In May, 1962, three months before I was to start school that following August, Mom took me to the last day of school picnic. It was for school children and families, although it was in the middle of the week so it was really just children and their mothers.

It would be an opportunity for me to meet some of the kids in the school. It was a very small school. At that time, there were maybe 30 kids in grades 1 through 8, and probably another dozen or so in high school. There were only two, three, or four kids to a class.

I didn't know anyone there except Lonnie. Our families went to the same church and our parents were long-time friends. Lonnie was a couple of years older than me. He always treated me with decency and never taunted me. Maybe he was a better friend than I realized.

I was scared that day, the day of the picnic. The school was in what seemed to be this huge brick building. There were at least four classrooms upstairs, and four downstairs.

The grade school classes met in two of the rooms upstairs. Grades 1 through 4 were in one room, and grades 5 through 8 were in another room. The high school occupied another couple of rooms upstairs, and downstairs were three or four more rooms.

The school building was big. At least to a five-year-old.

Outside was a playground with a swing and merry-go-round. An elm tree stood beside the swing. There was a field for softball.

And then there was the gymnasium, a separate building down the hill, close to the railroad tracks. That's where the high school boys played basketball and the girls

Urges by Gary Hennerberg

played volleyball. And there was a stage, too. That would be where we would have our music programs.

The school picnic was in the gymnasium. There were chairs for the grown-ups and we kids could climb up and down the bleachers which were built into the building.

After lunch, we went out to play. I wasn't very athletic, even though I was bigger than most of the kids my age. And I remember slowly walking around trying to figure out how to fit in.

It was my friend Lonnie who would call for me as he was hiding in the grass for a game of hide and seek. He was encouraging me to hide with him. At last, I was being invited to play!

So I ran toward him. But something bad happened. As I was running to join Lonnie, I slipped on the green grass, fell, and hit my elbow on a rock.

It hurt badly. And I cried a lot.

I remember walking slowly from the grassy knoll behind the school to the gymnasium to find Mom.

My elbow had swollen up quickly. I was still crying and it hurt. All I remember next is my Mom abruptly gathering the dishes she had brought for the picnic and we left.

The next thing I knew, we were at a doctor's office in the small town of Steele City, Nebraska, about five miles up the river from Hollenberg, Kansas. Steele City was only a little bigger than Hollenberg, but there was a doctor there.

He x-rayed my arm and concluded that I had cracked a bone. Then he put it in a cast. None of us were happy.

The drive back to the farm was long. And I remember wanting to show my Dad my cast. He was even less happy than me when he snapped, "Why did you go and do that."

I hadn't ever seen him so mad. But we were a poor farming family and I suppose as much as anything he was unhappy that there would be another bill to pay.

The cast came off a few weeks later and all was fine. But my first introduction to my school mates wasn't exactly what any of us had planned.

By August, the much anticipated first day of school had arrived.

My eyes still mist when I remember my Mom going through all my school supplies with me just before the school bus was to pick me up.

I can still hear her say, to this day, "And here are your scissors." She said it with a certain glee in her voice. It was like a foreshadowing that she knew then that those scissors would play a very important role in my life for the next 45 years, as you'll later read.

The school bus was small. Mom and I stood at the end of the driveway, perhaps 100 feet from our house.

Urges by Gary Hennerberg

> I can still hear her say, to this day, "And here are your scissors." She said it with a certain glee in her voice. It was like a foreshadowing that she knew then that those scissors would play a very important role in my life for the next 45 years.

We lived on a gravel county road, so it was somewhat more traveled than other roads. She stood with me as we looked to the South across the field and pasture up to the hill where Hollenberg was located. The town was on a bluff somewhat higher than where our house was located.

Suddenly the bus appeared over the hill a half mile away. The bright yellow made it unmistakable.

My heart raced with anticipation. I wasn't scared. I was looking forward to the day. While I don't recall anything else that happened that day, the memory of Mom giving me that pair of scissors stays etched in my mind.

⁓

I didn't make many friends in school. But Lonnie would continue to be a mentor for me through my school years. Sometimes he was a big brother to me that I didn't have.

4 — Blessings

His family lived about a mile away, across the section from our house. We could see their farmyard. They could see our farmyard. We would laugh when Lonnie's Mom would tell us in church that she saw us doing something.

Behind our house was a large pasture that shared a fence with their pasture. I remember one day when I was out in the pasture chopping thistles and I saw Lonnie and his younger brother Kevin in their pasture. We sat in the grass and talked for a while. Lonnie was in high school. The high school in Hollenberg had been consolidated with other schools while I was in grade school and now we had to go to Hanover, about 15 or so miles away. Lonnie told me about his experience in high school. It scared me.

He graduated in 1972. I graduated in 1974. We went our separate ways after graduating. He went to school and later worked construction building water towers.

One winter's day in 1978, when I was in college, I got a call that there had been an accident and Lonnie had fallen from a water tower. He died.

I ached for Lonnie's family. I was in college some 200 miles away and the day of his funeral I had another commitment. I struggled with what to do. In the end, I didn't go to Lonnie's funeral. It's a choice I regret to this day. He had been one of only a few childhood friends that had encouraged me that day back in 1961. I felt as if I had let him — and myself — down.

CHAPTER 5
Sequencing

You've heard the classic question: what came first, the chicken or the egg?

So I have to wonder what comes first. The euphoria from the anticipation of pulling my hair or the anxiety knowing it will leave a bigger bald spot.

I don't know that I ever looked forward to pulling my hair. There would have been too much deliberate thinking to have done that. Hair pulling was spontaneous for me. It would just sort of happen. A moment of intense thinking would prompt it. As does reading. Watching television. Even boredom.

Sometimes it was an automatic response. I would wake up in the morning and the first thing I would do is reach up and pull some hair. It was a way to wake up. It kick-started my brain for the day. Hair pulling first-thing in the morning was almost automatic. Sometimes it kept me in bed for a few more minutes while I pondered the upcoming day. Sometimes it was escape from a day I wasn't looking forward to.

But plucking some hair was a way to do what I wanted to do first. Then again, I'm not sure if I did it first because I liked it, or because I hated it so much.

Urges by Gary Hennerberg

The Carrot Lady was someone who appeared in my life for only a blink of time. I don't know her real name. I don't know where she was from. She came as a visitor to my school to talk about nutrition. But her message of the day resonated in many ways.

She was a petite woman with perfect posture. I remember her sitting prim and proper in a chair in our school room while all of us kids sat on the floor at her feet. I must have been in about the first or second grade.

She had her silver hair neatly pulled into a bun. She was impeccably dressed. And her voice had that grandmotherly kind of tone. A little shaky perhaps. But stern. She came across as tough as nails on the outside, but I bet she was a dear person on the inside.

> "Eat what you don't like first, and eat what you do like last."

Her lecture was about nutrition. She was an extraordinary role model for it and she really did call herself the "Carrot Lady." She seemed really old to me. Of course, to small kids anyone over age 40 is old.

I have no recollection of how long she talked. But the message I took away that day was abundantly clear:

"Eat what you don't like first, and eat what you do like last."

That's it. When you're eating, if you're served fried chicken, green beans and potatoes, but you don't like green beans, you should eat them first. Save what you like, say the fried chicken and potatoes, for later. And by all means, save dessert for last.

I've always remembered the Carrot Lady by how she regaled us that day about how to prioritize our eating habits. And I really can't say that I remember much of anything else about her except her simple, direct, and successfully delivered message. She left an impression on me that has never escaped my mind.

I have applied that philosophy of "do what you don't like first" to my life.

As an adult, I have adapted to and like most all foods. But when in doubt, I always eat what I don't like first.

Do you do what you like to do first? Or do you do what you don't like first?

When I'm working on projects, I carry through the same thought: I do what I don't like first. Then I finish with what I do like to do most. It's a reward.

This circles me back to hair pulling and a philosophy of life.

Urges by Gary Hennerberg

Do you do what you like to do first? Or do you do what you don't like to do first? Different perspectives, aren't they.

This may have nothing to do with anything for you. But I have to wonder.

As someone obsessed with doing the "don't like" before doing the "do like," I have to question how this has impacted me pulling my hair.

Wouldn't it seem that since hair pulling brings me such pleasure that I would do it last after doing what I don't like to do first?

I don't like the result of hair pulling, I like being in the trance of hair pulling. I like the adrenaline rush. The euphoria of the touch of my hair. Seeking out the perfect one or group to yank out. I like the split-second sensation of the hair coming out of my scalp. I'm fascinated by looking at my hair between my fingers that I could only otherwise see it in a mirror. In my hand, my hair is three-dimensional. I can see the color, the curl, the texture. And I can see the roots. White, with a spot of color at the very end. I can touch it. Feel the gliding motion while running my fingers from the top to the bump of the root. Ah! The rush! My heart races! I do it again. And again! There is no stopping it now!

5 — Sequencing

Then there is interruption. I pause. I stop. I look around at the devastation of my hair. A bigger bald spot. Another place where the skin on my scalp is soft and raw. Perfect to the touch. But wide open for the world to see.

So am I doing this in the order the Carrot Lady admonished me to do? Am I pulling first because I don't like it? Or am I pulling last because I do like it?

CHAPTER 6
Wiring

We're all wired differently. I visualize thousands — perhaps millions — of nerves and wires, microscopic in size that criss-cross my brain, a complicated weave of fabric that defines me.

I sense I have two wires crossed in my brain that produce this bizarre personality trait. The crossed wires have created a behavior over which I have no control. At one level, I'm obsessed with my appearance. I must be clean, neat, and well-dressed.

But at the other extreme, I love to pull my hair. I only pull with my left hand, even though I'm right handed. My left hand is like a robot acting independently from the rest of me. And while I know I'm pulling, something in my mind has given me permission to do it. It's euphoric. But when I come out of my trance, I go into depression with the sight of hair all over my shoulders and the floor.

I don't know why I do it. I'm powerless. But when I'm alone and it appears the world isn't watching, I raise my arm and sneak my hand onto my scalp, searching for the perfect

Urges by Gary Hennerberg

hair to pluck from my head. And when it's pulled, a rush of energy fills me.

No one needs to know. It's my little secret.

―⚬―

Even though we lived on a farm in Kansas — just a half mile from Nebraska — we considered ourselves Nebraskans. My Dad and Mom were raised on farms in Nebraska.

When we made a rare trip to Lincoln, Nebraska's state capital, it was usually to shop for something special that we couldn't find in the smaller town stores nearby. It took about 90 minutes to drive to Lincoln, and it was usually an all-day outing that I always looked forward to as a child.

If Mom and Dad told me why we were going to Lincoln one day, I don't remember it. I was probably 7 or 8 years old. It was summertime. I remember riding in the car with my parents as we traveled the narrow stretch of U.S. Highway 77 between Beatrice and Lincoln. The road was heavily traveled. The gentle rolling hills had their own beauty with the crops growing in the farm fields nearby.

I was always intrigued with a set of railroad tracks that paralleled the highway for a while, and the miles and miles of telephone and electric wires that ran from one community to another.

6 — Wiring

As we drove that day to Lincoln, I always looked forward to getting to the crest of a hill south of the city where you would suddenly see the Nebraska state capitol. It towered majestically above all the buildings in the city.

Coming into town, you would drive on 10th Street toward downtown and the capital area. A landmark and one of the stores where we would shop was Gold's Department Store. I can still hear the jingle from their radio and TV commercials. The words were something like "Gold's of Nebraska...has more of everything."

But that day we didn't stop at Gold's. We came to the main street in Lincoln, "O" Street, and turned east. We continued to drive for awhile before pulling into a parking lot outside a small building.

It was a doctor's office. I didn't know why we were there. Before I realized what was going on, I recall meeting with the doctor and his talking with us. Then I remember him looking at my scalp and moving my hair around. I closed my eyes and was paralyzed with fear. I didn't say a word.

He used a lighted instrument to go over my scalp as though the light would reveal something the naked eye couldn't see.

"It's not ringworm," I remember him telling my folks.

Of course it wasn't.

Silence followed as he kept looking around my scalp.

But then he asked me a question that is forever etched in my mind.

"Why do you pull your hair, son?"

My heart sank. And I didn't say a word.

I had been caught and I didn't know how to respond. How was it that he knew I pulled my hair? I hadn't done it in his presence. I never pulled when anyone was around me. How could Mom and Dad have known? I was so painstakingly careful to comb my hair over the bald spots that I thought no one knew.

> "Why do you pull your hair, son?" I had been caught and I didn't know how to respond.

That's all I remember of that day. He sent me out to the waiting room while he consulted with Mom and Dad.

That incident — the revelation of my hair pulling urge in front of my parents — was devastating. It was no longer a secret.

That was an era when we didn't know about repetitive body-focused disorders. I didn't know why I pulled my hair.

My parents had to have been frustrated and disappointed. And doctors didn't have a clue what to do.

6 — Wiring

Many years later, as an adult, when I discovered there are millions of people just like me, I shared my discovery with Mom and Dad. I think they were relieved. I can still hear my Dad's voice saying "We could never figure out why you pulled your hair."

When my parents read the draft of my book and this story, my Mom shared with me what the doctor told them that day. He told my parents they were giving too much attention to my sister who was four years younger than me. The doctor speculated that my desire to pull my hair was something I was doing for attention. That was nonsense. But back in the 1960s, no one knew what trich was or why children would pull hair.

> I have wondered what impact that doctor's misguided words had on my mother. Did it make her feel guilty? That somehow she was at fault?

I have wondered what impact that doctor's misguided words had on my mother. Did it make her feel guilty? That somehow she was at fault? There have been times when society would look at the mother of a child and blame her for that child's disorder. That's not fair to mothers. As a parent myself, I now know how little control we have over our kids, especially what they think, how they feel, and often what they do.

Urges by Gary Hennerberg

I still don't know why I pull my hair. But the reason why matters less to me as I get older. I've grown to accept that it simply "is." Yes, I rationalize that a wire is crossed somewhere in my brain. And perhaps that's true.

But that would be too easy of an explanation. The wires, the nerves, the blood vessels ... it's beyond comprehension. And most surely they cross each other. They zig, zag, and go every which way, transmitting thoughts and behaviors beyond our comprehension.

> I like to imagine that my brain could be opened up and that the one out-of-place wire could be lovingly moved to its proper place, the incision would be closed and I'd be normal for the rest of my life.

I like to imagine that my brain could be opened up and that the one out-of-place wire could be lovingly moved to its proper place, the incision would be closed and I'd be normal for the rest of my life. Or that a pill would make the wires fire properly. But that's not likely to happen. At least in my lifetime.

CHAPTER 7
Shame

Emotions can be like a roller coaster ride. One moment you're up, and another down.

The sensation and process of pulling hair is an up moment. First there is the touch of the hair. Sometimes the urges are to touch and stroke a hair then pull it out. Other times it's a quest to find a hair that shouldn't be there — a hair that is curlier than what I want. Or maybe it's grown in white from years of repeated pulling. Or it's coarser than most.

There has always been something about the texture of the hair that stimulated my urge to pull. I had naturally curly hair. I didn't always like the curls.

As my hand — always my left hand — would wander to my scalp, it would be with great anticipation of what I'd find and remove. There was usually a moment of comfort and peace, followed by anguish once I looked at the floor or in a mirror. Why was I on this roller coaster, and how could I get off of it? This roller coaster ride just was, and is. And from it came immense shame.

By the time I was about eight or nine, the pulling got worse. Instead of a small bald spot, I now had two sizeable spots I worked from. There was the bald spot above my left ear. Then later I pulled from my forehead to behind my ear. It was about an inch wide and probably three or more inches long.

One day I discovered that I enjoyed pulling more toward the top of my head. That spot grew and grew until it became about the size of a silver dollar.

Clearly, this problem wasn't subsiding and was only getting worse.

Mom and Dad never let on to me how they felt. They'd encourage me to stop, but I think they realized they were powerless over me. They wouldn't see me pull. It was always done in private. But they could see the depressing results.

Apparently they decided to see what would happen if my head was shaved.

The man who had cut my Dad's hair for years was named Noel. He and my Dad were about the same age and they had known each other since they were boys. I always thought Noel was a nice friendly man. And from the pictures I've seen of me when I was a child, I'd say he did a pretty good job of giving a haircut to a kid with bald spots.

But I wasn't prepared for what happened one day when my Dad gave Noel the orders to shave my head. I know Noel didn't want to do it.

7 — Shame

"Are you sure?" he asked my Dad. I just stared out the window. What's an eight- or nine-year-old to do when his Dad has given directions to another adult?

"Yeah," replied my Dad.

I knew what was up. It was an act of desperation from my Dad and Mom to do something to force me to quit pulling my hair. If it was all shaved off, there would be no way to pull.

But that only works if you shave the scalp every day. In a few days, my hair had grown out enough that I could pinch the end of the hair between the fingernail of my thumb and index finger. In fact, it wasn't long before I had developed a small callous on my index finger from the rigors of pulling.

Shaving my head didn't work. Before it was shaved, at least I could comb my hair over the bald spots and it wouldn't be seen. Well, okay, I have to admit it. It was probably not only obvious my hair was combed illogically, but that you could see the white scalp through strands of remaining hair.

But the result of shaving my head was even greater shame for what I

> Everyone could see the crudeness of what I had done to myself, yet there would be no way anyone could ever understand why. Including me.

did. Before my head was shaved at least I thought I was hiding it. Now I was completely exposed. Everyone could see the crudeness of what I had done to myself, yet there would be no way anyone could ever understand why. Including me.

Amazing how things change. Today I proudly sport a shaved head. Well, maybe not so proudly. I was just saying that. All things being equal, I'd rather have hair.

But as a 50-plus guy, I suppose it's possible I would have developed what happens to so many men: male pattern baldness.

Still, the 1960s and 1970s were an era when hair, especially long hair, was idolized. It was power. To me, having long hair created a certain cache when it was beautifully styled.

But now in the 21st century, it doesn't seem to matter if your hair is shaved or not. It's a look.

> The 1960s and 1970s were an era when hair, especially long hair, was idolized. It was power. To me, having long hair created a certain cache when it was beautifully styled.

7 — Shame

So perhaps that day in the 1960s when Dad had Noel shave my head it was a trend-setting day. But for a youngster who didn't want to be fast-forwarded to the 21st century, it was shame.

In retrospect, I wish that we — Mom, Dad and me — had figured out a way for me to keep my head shaved everyday instead of letting the hair grow out even a quarter of an inch. Even today, I can't let hair on my neck grow more than overnight before it's just barely long enough that I start to pull it.

I doubt shaving my head would have stopped me from pulling. There is no changing that urge. But perhaps I could have averted the huge and weirdly placed bald spots on my head today and not suffered so much shame as a child. I don't know. I never will.

Chapter 8
Compassion

The shame of pulling one's hair oppresses. It's a heavy burden because it never escapes you. A hair puller hides it and suffers in silence.

But there are multitudes of urges — some may call them issues — which most of us harbor inside. We take for granted that what we see on the outside appears to be a well adjusted human being. But what we don't know is that inside there are people who are tormented with something that eats away at their core.

As I look around at people, I sometimes wonder if a person I see has some type of compulsive urge or issue hidden inside of them. The reality is that I don't know. And most of us would never open up and disclose to anyone what's going on deep down within. You can't use a crowbar to pry open the human mind to see what's inside.

> We take for granted that what we see on the outside may appear to be a well adjusted human being. But what we don't know is that inside there are people who are tormented with something that eats away at their core.

Urges by Gary Hennerberg

But sometimes you can look at a person and tell if there is something wrong. Humans don't always know how to react to another person who has a handicap. We're afraid of looking at someone in a wheelchair. It makes us uncomfortable. Edgy. We don't want to deal with someone who doesn't seem normal. But every person has a story. And underneath the coat of armor that we as a human race put on to shield us from anyone attempting to penetrate our persona, we act as though nothing — nothing — is wrong with us. But not everyone, or every living thing, has that option.

> Every person has a story. And underneath the coat of armor that we as a human race put on to shield us from anyone attempting to penetrate our persona, we act as though nothing — nothing — is wrong with us.

⁂

Dad raised hogs for a few years, at a time when he could make some money doing it. Hogs weren't usually the livestock of his first choice.

Dad usually bought pigs when they were only a few weeks old and would then fatten them before selling them to the slaughterhouses. He wasn't terribly interested in breeding sows and then tending to the care required of a litter of baby pigs.

8 — Compassion

During the summer, when it was hot, the hogs would overheat and we'd have to cool them off. Or they would find a way to wallow in mud around the stock tanks to keep themselves cool. Usually the hogs had a way of splashing their drinking water out of the tank and in just a few minutes they would burrow and make a complete mess.

After school, it was my responsibility to fill the tanks with water.

I didn't like doing it.

After filling the tanks for awhile, I figured out about how long it would take to fill the tank to full. Usually I was right. And when I was wrong, well, let's just say I tended to err on the side of letting the water run too long. I don't know how the time would slip away. Sometimes it was because I'd try to sneak away and watch TV. Other times it was because I'd slip into a trance-like state from pulling my hair and lose complete track of time. Dad would get so mad at me when I'd "space-out" and let the tanks run over so the hogs could dig into the mud next to the stock tank.

But while we didn't raise baby pigs, one autumn Dad decided to keep sows and raise their litter.

So one day I went with him to the shed where he kept them to see a litter of new-born pigs. They were so clean. So white. Something you didn't normally see of pigs.

Urges by Gary Hennerberg

As Dad looked over the litter, he pulled out one of the baby pigs that was an obvious runt. It could never survive with all the other pigs competing for the sow's milk, so he said he would "knock it in the head," meaning he would do what seemed more humane than letting it starve to death.

I protested.

"Can't we save it? I'll take care of it myself!"

Dad paused for a moment, and then said I could care for it if I wanted to. But he warned me that it probably wouldn't live without its mother. That was a chance I was willing to take.

There was a small shed a few steps away that wasn't being used for anything. I could put the runt pig there. We got a bale of straw so the pig could sleep on it and stay warm, and then we found troughs for water. I honestly don't recall how I fed the pig, but we probably hand-fed it milk.

Of course, this pig needed a name. I called him Henry.

Remarkably, my "TLC" for Henry helped him pull through. He didn't die. He lived and grew bigger and bigger. He didn't grow as fast as his brothers and sisters since he was born the runt, but Henry became my pet and I fed him every day.

8 — Compassion

One day, after Henry was several weeks old, it came to my attention that Henry was not a "he." Henry was a "she." I'd have to change the name. But that was easy. I decided to call her Henrietta. And so it was.

After a few months Henrietta grew up to be a big healthy full grown hog. She was tame, not like the other hogs that wouldn't let you pet them. I could go into her pen and stroke the top of her head for a few seconds, and she'd nuzzle my leg with her nose.

While she became a pet of sorts, the fact was that she was a hog. I always knew that. And I always knew that someday she would be grown up and ready for market. Unlike a dog or cat, I wouldn't be able to keep her throughout her entire life.

I was saddened when we took her to market, but Dad rewarded me for all the work I had done to raise her. He gave me $100, and I beamed with pride when we walked into the bank in Fairbury so I could open my very first savings account.

I had earned the money. And along the way I had done a good deed. Henrietta wouldn't have made it on her own without my intervention.

Those of us who live with bizarre urges need nurturing, too. I pull my hair. Many people have urges that they can't

Urges by Gary Hennerberg

control. Whether it's skin picking, an eating disorder, gambling, hoarding, or one of surely dozens — perhaps hundreds — of urges, we may be looked upon as the "runt" of the litter.

We all need tender loving care. And I'd suggest that some of us need more TLC than others.

Henrietta couldn't help it that she was born a runt. Had I not saved her, she wouldn't have survived. With special care, she grew up to be a healthy animal.

I think that's how it is with people who harbor urges in their soul. We need a little extra attention to get us through those early years of our lives when the external forces around us can be so cruel.

> Some of us may actually work through our urges. Others of us don't ever escape the urges. We live with them and carry those bizarre thoughts in our minds for our entire lives.

Some of us may actually work through our urges. Others of us don't ever escape the urges. We live with them and carry those bizarre thoughts in our minds for our entire lives.

For the hair puller, we live lives of shame through our baldness. We comb our hair differently, we buy wigs and hairpieces, or we wear caps, scarves and hats.

8 — Compassion

For the skin picker, clothes and make-up are used to hide the physical scars.

For the person whose urge is to overeat, they live lives shuttered away from others as morbidly obese individuals. For the person who eats and purges, they outwardly seem so healthy until the years of abuse catch up with them.

> You can't always recognize the person who needs TLC. Most of us carry our burdens by ourselves, hidden in silence.

The person whose urge it is to gamble goes silently and under the radar, depriving them of fully enjoying the money they work to make.

And so it goes. You can't always recognize the person who needs TLC. Most of us carry our burdens by ourselves, hidden in silence. The world could be a much more compassionate place than it is. There is sometimes the attitude that only the fittest or strongest survive. But doesn't everyone — the Henrietta's of the world — deserve a chance to live full lives, too?

CHAPTER 9
Church

Our family was a family of church goers and we rarely missed a Sunday at church. It was a good habit instilled early in my life. Without my faith it would have been more difficult for me to accept my urge to pull hair.

My faith was my path. I could have blamed God for giving me this mysterious disorder. I could have given up on God when my prayers went unanswered. But I didn't.

It would have been easy to have given up on my faith, too. Without my faith, I would have been lost. So I clung to it, knowing that there was a plan for me. I never gave up on that belief. It is what has ultimately led me to writing this book.

Several years ago, I had a powerful feeling come to me that brought clarity to me for my mission on this earth. That was for me to be a role model for other hair pullers and people with compulsive disorders. A role model who could illustrate to children that it was possible to grow

> Without my faith, I would have been lost. So I clung to it, knowing that there was a plan for me. I never gave up on that belief.

Urges by Gary Hennerberg

up to be normal with normal relationships and careers. The inspiration to write this book came because I had achieved some semblance of normalcy. And, that through writing this book, I would discover things about myself that I didn't know. Writing would restore memories of events that together had served to mold me into the person I am today. I could break my silence because I was comfortable speaking to people. I could be a "face" of trich and illustrate that trichotillomania isn't a terrible mental illness.

> I let trich limit me for most of my life. I held myself back. If I could go back in time and do things over, it would have been to accept trichotillomania as part of my life and to have moved on. To have openly talked about it with those who were curious. To have ended suffering alone and in silence.

Through my words, I could be a messenger for those who struggle with trich. Today I can shrug it off as nothing more than hair pulling. Yeah, it's strange. I didn't want to have it. But trich will only limit you if you let it.

I let trich limit me for most of my life. I hid behind the shame. I didn't engage in certain activities. I held myself back. If I could go back in time and do things over, it would have been to accept trichotillomania as

9 — Church

part of my life and to have moved on. To have openly talked about it with those who were curious. To have ended suffering alone and in silence.

⟨⊙⟩

My childhood church was named Zion Lutheran Church. The land for the church, parsonage and cemetery had been donated by my great-grandparents in 1910.

The church was built on the crest of a gentle hill on the Kansas side of the state line road. The church faced toward Nebraska. The roads going from Nebraska into Kansas didn't exactly align. It appeared that when surveyors over a century ago carved out sections of land — 640 acres in a square mile when the West was settled — that they didn't confer with the neighboring state on their boundaries.

But the road from the north, on the Nebraska side, pointed directly toward the church on the Kansas side. There was a "T" in the road. To continue heading south into Kansas, a driver would have to make a 90 degree turn to the west for a couple of hundred feet, then veer 90 degrees back to the south.

The cemetery was located at the corner of the other "T" to the west of the church. There was a small native prairie field of grass between the church and the cemetery. We didn't go there unless there was a funeral or it was Memorial Day, or "Decoration Day" as my Grandmother would call it.

I never knew my great-grandparents — my father's mother's parents — who had donated the land. They died in the 1940s, just days apart from each other and they are buried in the church cemetery.

My grandmother grew up in that church. My grandparents were married there. They raised their five boys there, my Dad and his brothers.

I was baptized at that church as an infant in 1956 and confirmed in 1970. I have many fond memories of that church.

When the church was first constructed, a parsonage had been built for the pastor to live in. In those days, the pastor usually served only one church. But in the 1950s, our church started to share a pastor with the Lutheran Church in Lanham, a small community just a few miles to the east on the state line. The pastor would live in Lanham. The residence was later converted into a Parish Hall for Sunday School classes.

While there was electricity to our church out on the prairie, there wasn't running water. There was an outhouse toward the back of the property for emergency use. Thankfully Church services and Sunday School only lasted a couple of hours.

9 — Church

This church was, and continues to be, an anchor for me. As I write this book, State Line Lutheran Church is still there after nearly a century of existence. I understand there are only a handful of people, many of them my extended family, who still attend Sunday worship there. I hope it's always there, but the realities of dwindling populations in that part of the country make it unlikely it will always be there, even during my lifetime.

There were two events every year at that church that I cherished: Vacation Bible School in the summer and the Christmas Eve program put on by those of us in children's Sunday School.

Bible School was a weeklong program, usually following the Memorial Day weekend right after school was finished for the school year. It always seemed so vibrant and alive to me.

It was the Christmas Eve service that was always my favorite. It was a program put on by us kids in Sunday School. We would practice every Sunday afternoon for the month of December rehearsing our lines and singing our songs. Sometimes I would sing a solo.

On Christmas Eve, before the program, we would all assemble in the Parish Hall. We would put on red and white capes made by our mothers and grandmothers. We would each be given candles. Then when the program was to begin, we would line up and walk the 40 or so

Urges by Gary Hennerberg

feet outside from the Parish Hall to the Church. Once inside the church, our candles would be lit and we would process down the aisle singing *O Come All Ye Faithful*. That's how every Christmas Eve service began.

The church was also the site of some sad occasions. My grandparents' funerals were there, and they are buried in the church cemetery near my great-grandparents. There were other funerals over the years of family and neighbors. And while those moments were sad, I have always believed in the saving grace of Jesus Christ. And while our bodies may be taken away from this earth, our spirits are freed and live on.

We all need faith and something to believe in. How else do we manage to get through the toils of daily living?

Going to church has been a lifelong habit for me. It has been a place to reconnect with God. I've never blamed God for trichotillomania, although I've wondered why it exists. Just as I've wondered why all the bad things in Mother Nature exist.

> So much of this journey has been acceptance and faith. Acceptance that I am who I am, and faith that God has created me as part of a bigger plan.

But so much of this journey has been acceptance and faith. Acceptance that I am who I am, and faith that God has created me as part of a bigger plan.

As a child, I had always wondered why God wouldn't answer my prayers and make me stop pulling my hair. We were taught that "God answers prayer." Well, God didn't stop me. But I later came to realize that not all prayers are "answered." Now I pray that prayers are "heard." Because when they are heard, God is listening. And when God is listening, we as humans open our mind to possibilities, and discover guidance and answers to our hopes and dreams.

CHAPTER 10
Strength

Strengths and talents are often deeply woven into our fabric. I wonder if God does that so that we embark on a lifelong journey of discovery.

I think that God gives every one of us multitudes of talents just waiting to be discovered. Imagine continual "a-ha!" moments about yourself for your entire life. Many of us discover what we're good at doing early in life. Then I think "life" takes over and the discoveries are happenstance. Perhaps a self awareness takes over later, but I wonder if later in life we're just tired and the discovery ends.

Discovering talents early in life is essential for children. I think parents

> I think that God gives every one of us multitudes of talents just waiting to be discovered. Imagine continual "a-ha!" moments about yourself for your entire life.

have a responsibility to expose their children to as many activities as possible. It enables them to find things they like to do, and to build teamwork and social skills. Some of us thrust our kids into sports activities. For others, it's music, dance, theater or the like. It doesn't always matter what children are exposed to doing, because it is the involvement with others that brings talent to the surface. It develops responsibility and social skills.

My motivation to become involved in an activity was inspired by the idea that if I could distract myself from pulling my hair, that somehow I would magically stop doing it. For I knew then that when I was busy, especially keeping my hands active, that I wouldn't reach up to my scalp and begin another pulling frenzy.

> Along the journey of distracting myself from my compulsions — my demons — I discovered talents that have served me well throughout my life.

But along the journey of distracting myself from my compulsions — my demons — I discovered talents that have served me well throughout my life. And they helped me grow up just a little faster, too.

When I was 8 years old I wanted to join 4-H. Other kids I knew were joining, and age 8 was the youngest a child could become a member. But Mom and Dad thought I should wait. So when I turned 9, they let me become a member. I suspect one of the reasons Dad let me join 4-H is that he realized I would learn skills that would serve me well on the farm.

Our 4-H Club was named Joy Creek, after a creek that ran through our township and the farm of our club leaders.

4-H was, and still is today, an organization for youth and teens. Back in the 1960s when I first joined, there were clubs in each township in the county where members would take on a specific project. One of the projects in which we could enroll included learning about livestock. There were other pursuits such as cooking, woodworking and photography.

The four "H's" stood for head, heart, hands and health. 4-H was designed to be an experience for young children that would enrich our minds, make us more compassionate, help us discover our talents, and maintain good health. We were taught to be responsible citizens. And one of the requirements of being a member was to pursue one or more projects.

My first year's project was dairy. I have to admit that I don't know why I selected dairy. At the time I joined 4-H, which would have been around 1965 or 1966, my Dad milked cows so it was easy to let my dairy project blend in with the rest of the farm operation.

Dad had a small herd of dairy cows, maybe 30. They were all Holsteins. Holsteins are a popular breed of cow

Urges by Gary Hennerberg

for producing milk. They weather the warm and cold of extreme Midwestern temperatures and consistently produce abundant supplies of milk. If you don't know what a Holstein looks like, well, they're black and white. Their markings are like our fingerprints. It seems there are no two Holsteins that look exactly alike. Usually the markings are random. I wouldn't say they are pretty. But sometimes you'll find a Holstein cow with markings that make her a nice sight to see.

> One of the things 4-H did was to help me discover a talent I didn't know that I had. It's a talent that has served me well in my life even though it is a contradiction for me.

4-H did more for me than I could have ever realized while growing up. One of the things 4-H did was to help me discover a talent I didn't know that I had. It's a talent that has served me well in my life even though it is a contradiction for me.

Through 4-H, I discovered that I'm unafraid of talking in front of an audience. I relish the moment. It's an adrenalin rush for me. Not all that different, I suppose, from the adrenalin rush I experience when I pull my hair. I've never really understood how standing up in front of a crowd can be rated as one of people's biggest fears.

I admit to multiple inconsistencies here. I'm obsessed with my appearance. At one time in my life I had a complete fear of someone discovering my hair pulling secret. Yet I enjoy being in front of people even though there is a risk they would see my bald spots. That's living on the edge.

I've pondered this dichotomy, among others in my life, many times. I didn't become involved in sports because I was afraid someone would see that I have bald spots when my hair could be messed up during the action of the game. There were plenty of coaches who wanted me to play basketball and football because of my size and height, but in addition to not being terribly athletic, I didn't want a discovery made about my deep dark hair pulling secret.

I prefer to blend in with the crowd as much as I can. But I keep reminding myself to celebrate my height and let people be drawn to my physical presence.

I enjoy being in front of an audience today. Maybe it was one, single positive experience early in my life that has given me that ease to give a speech or presentation.

The 4-H experience was an outstanding one. As I recall, I joined in the fall, or maybe winter, after I turned 9. That first March, in 1966, would be a public speaking experience that I still fondly remember and cherish. It did my heart and mind good.

Urges by Gary Hennerberg

That March of '66 there was an all-day Saturday event called County Club Days. On that day, 4-H members from the dozen or so 4-H clubs in Washington County would gather in Washington, Kansas, the county seat, to participate in various activities and presentations.

As 4-H members, we were all encouraged to participate in at least one event.

Since my 4-H project was dairy, I decided to give a Project Talk based on dairy. I didn't have a dairy heifer yet of my own, but I was learning about dairy cattle. I read the 4-H materials about what constitutes a dairy heifer worthy of recognition when being judged in competition. For this Project Talk, I would be given a few minutes — 5 to 10 as my memory recalls — to stand before a judge and give my memorized presentation.

I had never given a Project Talk before. But our club leader — her name was Versa — encouraged me to do it. She had a plastic model of a Holstein cow that stood about a foot tall. She let me use it. I don't know how she came by this model, but it was of the perfect Holstein in appearance and build. The Holstein in the model was tall, firm, and with the ideal size udder for producing an abundant supply of milk.

I researched everything for my Project Talk from the 4-H manuals. I wrote my own speech. I practiced it over and over again. And I quickly memorized it. Funny how easy it is as a youngster to memorize a speech when you don't have all the noise we adults carry around, eventually leaving us unable to remember the simplest details of life.

I had anticipated the day of my Project Talk for weeks. And finally that cold March day arrived. I dressed in my best school clothes so I would look nice or at least as presentable as a 9 year-old with bald spots could look. And I made sure to have my model Holstein.

The drive to Washington took about 20 minutes from our farm. The high school was on the north side of town. It was a new school and it seemed so big to me. We checked in to see what room I was to give my talk. I had been assigned a time, but I don't recall when it was. I think it was mid-morning. But we arrived in plenty of time for me to practice and deliver my Project Talk.

There weren't usually too many people in the audience. Mom was there for sure. Versa, the club leader was there. I think she was proud of me. Or maybe she gave me special attention because she knew that I was hiding this horrific hair pulling habit and my self esteem was in shambles. There may have been a few other interested parties in the room, too. But importantly there was the judge. I didn't know his name or what qualified him to be a judge for a Project Talk, but he was the person making the decision of whether I would earn a blue ribbon (the

Urges by Gary Hennerberg

highest honor), a red ribbon, or a white ribbon (the lowest rating).

I stood in front of the classroom with a desk beside me where I placed the model Holstein. I remember pointing to the model and explaining to the audience what one should look for in an outstanding heifer. I talked about the head shape. The neck length. The straightness of the back. The front legs. The back legs. And the udder, a key point. After all, we raised Holsteins for the milk they produced. I remember being a little embarrassed about pointing to the udder. It seemed so, uh, personal.

> After my Project Talk, almost everyone in the audience came up to me and told me what a great job I had done. It boosted my self-confidence and gave me a new feeling of self-worth during a time when I was struggling with the shameful urge to pull my hair. ⌒

Maybe it was the charm in the innocence of a 9 year-old that captured everyone's hearts that day. After my Project Talk, almost everyone in the audience came up to me and told me what a great job I had done. I must have been walking on clouds. It boosted my self-confidence and gave me a new feeling of self-worth during a time when I was struggling with the shameful urge to pull my hair.

It would be awhile before I'd learn how the judge had rated me. There wasn't a formal announcement. Rather, on a board in the lobby there was a list of everyone's names. Someone would write on the board what ribbon each contestant had won. It took a few hours for all the Project Talks to be delivered. So we went to listen to other Project Talks, Demonstrations, and other presentations that morning to wait out the results.

The results must have been posted while we were in someone else's session, because when we stepped out of the auditorium into the lobby, there were crowds around the lists of names.

We politely waited our turn to get closer to the board. Mom let me go up and look for myself.

"I got a blue ribbon!" I said. I didn't shout. But I was overjoyed! But Mom inched closer to look for herself. Later, Versa, our club leader, would accumulate the ribbons for everyone in our club to present to us later.

> "I got a blue ribbon!"

I don't know where that blue ribbon is anymore. Nor does it matter to me, because the memory of that day is something I have cherished for my entire life.

Urges by Gary Hennerberg

This would be a day that made a difference in my life. It was a day that I could have a small triumph and discover that speaking in front of an audience wasn't something to be afraid of. I had discovered a God-given strength I would be able to use for the rest of my life.

Everyone needs a boost to their self-confidence. This isn't to be confused with ego. A healthy ego is a good thing. It permits a person to be confident and to know what they are good at doing. We've all witnessed big egos that aren't terribly healthy. Sometimes the improperly cultivated ego breeds arrogance. That's when people turn against you instead of cheer for you.

Then there is humility. That's an emotional reality check. So when I need to bring myself back to earth, I remind myself of that day at County Club Days, when the people in that room wanted this 9 year-old to get the blue ribbon. Life is better when there are people on the sidelines cheering us on to win.

Chapter 11
Unconditional Love

Unconditional love is a wonderful thing. There were times when I was growing up that I wondered how my Mom and Dad could ever love a child who pulled his hair. While they may not have always expressed their love of me in words, they expressed their love to me in praise, affirmation and actions.

Mom and Dad knew I pulled my hair before I realized that they knew. For some time, I thought I had done a great job of hiding it and no one had a clue. But parents know more than we give them credit for.

> It would have been easy for Mom and Dad to have constantly reminded me of my hair pulling urge. But to their credit, they didn't say much about it to me.

It would have been easy for Mom and Dad to have constantly reminded me of my hair pulling urge. But to their credit, they didn't say much about it to me.

It would have been easy for them to have berated me for pulling my hair. But, again, to their credit, they didn't.

Instead, I now realize that one thing they gave me was a lot of praise and words of affirmation. They told me I was smart. They said positive things to me.

In the book Five Love Languages by Gary Chapman, he outlines five "languages" that we use to express love and how we like to receive love. His book is mostly for adults in relationships, but he notes how it applies to children, too.

In a workbook of Chapman's, he has created a profile to help the reader understand the primary language in which we receive love. I was surprised when I took the test. It revealed that the primary way love can be expressed to me is through words of affirmation.

When I heard Chapman during one of his recorded presentations, it was apparent how his principles apply to children, too. I knew in an instant that perhaps unbeknownst to my parents, they were communicating love to me in the best way that they could.

My parents knew that there was nothing — absolutely nothing — they could do to stop me from pulling out my hair. And when I think about that, it must have taken a great deal of restraint for my parents to let nature take its course and let me go on and disfigure myself.

In the 1960s and 70s, we didn't know then what we do today about trichotillomania. A strong emotional response for many of us who pull our hair is shame. As I was growing up, perhaps it was easier to not talk about it because we didn't

11 — Unconditional Love

know what to do. And at the time, it seemed to me, and to my parents, that I was the only child in the universe who pulled hair. There was no one to go to for help. No magic treatment. Nothing that could be done.

Today I know that they loved me despite the fact that I pulled my hair. They loved me enough to know that by nagging at me to stop it would only make it worse. Rather, they heaped words of praise — affirmations — that are important to me still today.

> A parent's greatest gift to their child is unconditional love.

Love can heal wounds. One of God's greatest gifts to us is to give and feel love. And a parent's greatest gift to their child is unconditional love.

4-H became an important part of my childhood. Once I had demonstrated to my Dad and Mom that I was serious about 4-H, they reciprocated by seriously supporting me in my dairy project.

It would have been easy for my Dad to have given me a newborn calf from one of the cows in his herd for my dairy project. But he wanted me to have a heifer that would be worthy of showing at the County Fair.

That spring, after giving my project talk at County Club Days, I didn't know that Dad was looking for a heifer

Urges by Gary Hennerberg

for my dairy project until one day when we got in the truck and drove to a dairy farm about 40 miles away. He had been looking for a young heifer that I could call my own, and he found one that came from good breeding stock. She was a registered Holstein complete with the papers of her lineage.

Her name, given by the people who sold her to us, was Whimpie. She was beautiful. She was relatively tame, obviously groomed to be a show animal by the owners. She was only a few months old and had a lot of growing up to do.

And she was to be my new pet — really more like my new pal — for the next few years.

I grew to love Whimpie. I think Mom and Dad did, too.

Every day that spring and summer I would carefully put on her halter, making sure to perfectly loop it around her head, ears and mouth so it was comfortable for her. Then I would lead her around the barnyard to practice as I prepared to show her at the fair.

By July, our 4-H club's monthly meeting would be a "club tour" to every member's farm to see our club projects. I had never done that before since it was my first year in 4-H and I didn't know what to expect. It was a Sunday afternoon, and we all met at one of the other member's farm. We would spend just a few minutes looking at someone's project, usually cattle, hogs, or a garden, and then we would all caravan to another member's farm a short distance away.

I was a little nervous about everyone coming to our place. But the day before I had washed Whimpie, spending extra time to wash out the grass stains from her knees from when she would lay down. Her hooves required some extra polishing, too.

That Sunday morning after church, and before we left to begin the tour, I brushed her so she would look good. I was so proud of her. We moved her to a pen near the driveway so I could quickly bring her out to show everyone when they arrived.

The hour finally came when we all drove to our farmyard. There were probably a dozen cars in our driveway. I had never seen so many cars at our place. It made me feel important. After all, they all drove to our farm to see my 4-H project: Whimpie.

While everyone was either parking or getting out of the cars, I went to a pen to get Whimpie. No one had ever seen her before. Her shoulder was about the height of my shoulder.

I spoke for a minute about how I cared for her and that I was looking forward to showing her at the county fair in a couple of weeks. While I was talking, she surprised me by moving a little bit, enough that she would lift her

Urges by Gary Hennerberg

front leg off the ground and she stomped on my foot. That hurt. But I kept on talking, and then I lead her in a circle for everyone to see her. It was a successful day.

The club tour was one more opportunity to rehearse showing Whimpie before the county fair.

I was excited about preparing for the fair. It meant I had to pack a trunk to take along her halter, rope, shampoo, brushes and bucket so I could water her, and of course, we had to take hay and grain to feed her. Whimpie would be staying overnight for two nights in a big barn with all the other cattle from 4-H members from across the county.

When the day for the fair finally arrived, I was so excited. We loaded Whimpie in the truck and drove to Washington. Of course, when we arrived, there were a few dozen other 4-H members unloading their cattle, hogs and sheep. I don't recall the logistics of that process, but something tells me it was a bit nerve-wracking for my Dad who had to maneuver the truck in the lot so we could unload Whimpie, the trunk, hay and grain.

The barn had entrances on two sides. Once you walked in, you would walk up and down aisles where we were assigned a stall. There was straw on the floor which served two practical uses. First, it was a place for the cattle to lie down. But second, when Mother Nature called and cows would have to relieve themselves, it meant the straw would soak up the urine and by using a pitchfork, solid waste could be picked up and taken outside to a disposal wagon.

Judging took place the first day. The judge would award ribbons based on his evaluation of the cow's physical characteristics, how well it was groomed, along with the attention of the boy or girl who was showing the dairy cow.

A blue ribbon was the best, followed by red, then white ribbons. And there would also be a Grand Champion purple ribbon awarded.

I was nervous. Some of the other kids who were showing their dairy heifer were much older than me and had done it for many years.

Before leading Whimpie outside to the area where we would walk our cows in a circle, I brushed her one more time. I made sure her halter was on just right. Then I untied the rope and lead her outside.

I didn't really know what I was supposed to do beyond keeping her head close to my body and walk her in the circle.

We walked around the pen a few times. It seemed like it took a long time, but it probably all passed in less than 10 minutes. The judge then had us all line up and he made the announcements.

Urges by Gary Hennerberg

I had won a blue ribbon! I was so proud. But what the judge said next I didn't quite understand. He went to award the Grand Champion ribbon to one of the other recipients, but he went on to announce that Whimpie really was most deserving of the Grand Champion award.

I hadn't watched the judge and didn't see him signaling me to move to the front of the line. I had been penalized for watching Whimpie instead of the judge.

> My joy of winning a blue ribbon was cut to nothing when I learned that I could have won the Grand Champion.

I was heartbroken. My joy of winning a blue ribbon was cut to nothing when I learned that I could have won the Grand Champion.

Dad was so disappointed. But he didn't say much to me. Perhaps he knew that harsh words wouldn't change a thing and that had I known to watch the judge, I would have been doing it.

It was a painful lesson. But I still loved Whimpie. It wasn't her fault that I had missed the judge's cue.

Over the years I would show her again at the County Fair. I never got the Grand Champion. The next year I received another Blue Ribbon. But as Whimpie got older, she didn't show as well. Ultimately the best that we could win after a couple of years was a Red Ribbon.

11 — Unconditional Love

It was time to retire Whimpie from showing. By that time she had gone on to become an adult cow and had her own calves. We milked her for years and years. She became less and less of a pet and just another cow. Dad sold all of his dairy cows a few years later, but we held back Whimpie. Mom decided that she would milk Whimpie so that we could have fresh milk to drink and for cooking. I would milk her occasionally, too, but usually I was helping Dad with other farm chores.

Eventually it got to be too much to keep milking Whimpie every morning and night and we gave her to my uncle Ervin who had a large herd of dairy cows. It made much more sense for him to milk her with all the others. Whimpie probably enjoyed the company of other cows, too. Well, I don't really know about that. But that's what I told myself. It was painful to let go of my Grand Champion, my pet, and my pal.

―⁂―

Unconditional love is such a strong emotion. It is the strongest gift you can give to someone, be it your mate, your children, and your parents.

I was so fortunate to have been given the parents who would nurture me in my life. I still believe in my soul that God put me in their hands because he knew that I was going to take a special kind of love.

Urges by Gary Hennerberg

Perhaps my parents knew those words of affirmation would be what I needed to thrive. Or perhaps they could see that I responded so well to their praise.

But those affirming words would never stop my hair pulling. Mom and Dad had to have hoped that someday a miracle would happen and I would mysteriously stop pulling my hair. But they had the wisdom to recognize it wouldn't do any good to tell me or nag at me to stop.

Over the years, as I've met other hair pullers at conferences and the parents of teenagers, I've had the opportunity to tell those parents that the greatest gift they can give their child is love. Tell them you love them. Demonstrate that you love them. Be a great role model. And love them unconditionally no matter what happens.

> The greatest gift they can give their child is love. Tell them you love them. Demonstrate that you love them. And love them unconditionally no matter what happens.

CHAPTER 12

Looping

Rituals are hard to understand. Combine the ritual with a repetitive action and the action goes over and over again, almost as if in a loop.

I've met many hair pullers over the years. And we share something in common.

> Hair pulling is a ritual. Some may say a habit, but to me it's a ceremony.

Hair pulling is a ritual. Some may say a habit, but to me it's a ceremony.

The action of pulling is stimulating. It's the euphoria of having found the perfect hair to expel from your body. The one that seems to have a different texture. Maybe a different curl or coarseness that makes it unworthy to stay atop the head.

The tug or yanking action doesn't require great strength. Just a quick snap and it's out. Ah. I can feel the adrenalin rush. Whether real or imagined, I sense the quickness of my heart rate, my blood flowing faster, and an immediate sense of pleasure. Oh, it feels so-o-o good.

But the ritual isn't over. No, there's more to come. I want to see this hair in my hand, grasped tightly between my left index finger and thumb. Ah yes. That nasty hair is out! Just what I thought! It curls. I don't like curls on my head. It feels different and it doesn't belong there. I'm glad it's out.

Just look at that root. White with a black dot at the very end, at the core, deepest within my scalp. Closest to my brain, the nerves, the blood supply.

Sometimes there would be a trace of blood on the end of the root. A special one, indeed!

And the ritual would continue.

I would hold the hair with my fingers, and then put the roots to my lips. The roots were always cool to the touch. A dichotomy I don't understand. Why are the roots of hair cool to the touch when they were so deeply embedded in my scalp and should have the same body temperature as the rest of me? It deserved to go.

But I wasn't finished yet with this hair. After touching it to my lips, sometimes I liked to strip the root from the hair and look more deeply at the composition of the root. And sometimes I just dispensed with it, dropping it to the floor.

There. It's gone. Eradicated from my head.

Now on to finding the next one.

I love the smell of freshly cut alfalfa. The first crop of the spring season was always greeted with mixed anticipation. I loved the scent, and loved cutting and raking the hay. But baling it and stacking the bales in the

12 — Looping

barn? I didn't particularly enjoy that, but doing it taught me many valuable lifelong lessons.

It took planning to cut, rake, bale and stack hay. Before making the decision to cut alfalfa — the hay we'd feed to cattle during the winter months — we had to make sure the weather would be good for at least three days. The first day would be reserved for mowing. The second for raking. And the third day was for baling. Rain on the alfalfa after mowing it risked that it would mold and the cattle wouldn't eat it. Worse, if baled and put in the barn wet, through chemical processes I can't explain, it would get warm — sometimes hot — and while rare, it could get so hot that it would later burn.

Cutting hay would begin first thing in the morning. Sometimes the night before cutting hay, we would hook up the mower to the tractor. Getting the tractor and mower ready didn't take a lot of time, but the preparation was all-important.

The tractor needed fuel before going to the field. There was fresh ice and water to be put in a jug for drinking so I wouldn't dehydrate. Then there was driving to the field.

The path behind the barn was definitely the road not taken very often. There was a narrow opening between the barn and the windbreak of trees. I always admired those trees. Actually, I mostly appreciated the fact that

Urges by Gary Hennerberg

someone generations before me planted several rows of trees. Those trees would shield our home and farm yard from the cold northern winter winds.

After passing between the barn and trees, the landscape would open up to an expanse of fertile fields to my left, and ahead of me were the rolling hills of the pasture. In about 100 feet, I would make a 90 degree turn to my left and drive along the barbed wire fence separating the cattle from the crops. After another 300 feet or so, I'd make another 90 degree turn to the right. It was at that turn I was always intrigued with a lone tree. It wasn't a large tree. Probably a mulberry tree, but there it stood all by itself, probably the by-product of a bird having eaten a mulberry seed and, let's just say, deposited it there while taking a break on the barbed wire of the fence.

Mowing the alfalfa was a process: stop the tractor, put it in neutral and apply the brake, drop the mower to the ground, and then hop off the tractor to unhook the sickle and gently guide it to the ground. The sickle dropped to the right rear of the tractor.

Setting the tractor gear and speed correctly was important. The engine had to be revved up high enough for it to run the mower at a fast enough speed to cut the alfalfa, and the gear had to be slow enough so the tractor didn't move too fast.

12 — Looping

Mowing was therapeutic. I enjoyed watching the alfalfa, usually around a foot to two feet tall with lush green stems and vibrant purple blooms, cascade to the ground once it was cut. But it was the fresh spring smell of the alfalfa that made the morning sunshine even sweeter.

After mowing the alfalfa, it had to be raked. Usually we raked the day after we mowed. If it was unusually hot and dry, it might be raked later that same day.

Dad had a special way he wanted the alfalfa raked. He liked long rows that didn't go over terraces. And the amount of alfalfa raked into multiple rows throughout the field needed to be just right for the baler to bale at an optimum speed.

> I enjoyed watching the alfalfa, usually around a foot to two feet tall with lush green stems and vibrant purple blooms, cascade to the ground once it was cut.

Baling hay was hard work. So was putting the baled hay in the barn. It was demanding physical work, usually done when it was hot outside, and the dust from the hay — by now it had cured from mowing and raking — wasn't pleasant. While the wonderful scent of alfalfa still lingered, the sparkle was off the bloom with the hard work of baling.

Urges by Gary Hennerberg

When I was a child - before I was old enough to mow and rake the hay - baling hay was a family job. My paternal grandfather would drive the tractor. My Dad and uncles would stack the hay on the hayrack — a trailer pulled behind the baler — where one or two of the men would stand and catch bales. One guy doing it was sufficient, but two was better, especially when Grandpa would kick the tractor in a higher gear!

As a child, I usually stood at the back of the hayrack out of the way of my Dad or uncles. My Uncle Dennis was only nine years older than I was. I didn't have any brothers, so Dennis was almost like an older brother to me.

Dennis would catch the bales as they came out of the baler. He was also the "eye" watching the baler to see if it ran out of string or missed tying a bale. When that happened, he would wave and yell at Grandpa and things would come to a stop.

Back on the hayrack, Dennis taught me a system for stacking the bales. They had to criss-cross to create a sturdy load. When Grandpa made a quick stop, turned a corner, or went over a terrace, the entire load would sway back and forth. It was imperative that the load be secure, or we'd have to stop and pick up bales that had fallen off the hayrack to the ground.

12 — Looping

Stacking the bales was like building a foundation. And Dennis and I would often challenge ourselves to see how many bales we could stack on a hayrack. It was usually 80 to 100. But sometimes we'd make it a giant load. I'd get on top of the bales and he would throw bales up to me. I loved that.

Then there was stacking the bales in the barn. The first crop in springtime meant surveying the barn to decide where to start stacking hay first. The first hayrack load of hay could often be unloaded by pulling the trailer next to the barn. Here is where my Dad and Uncle Ervin usually stacked hay during the day while Uncle Dennis and I were in the field. Sometimes my Uncle Lyle and cousin Jerry helped us, as well. We could get more done with three or four hayracks. One was in the field being loaded, another was being unloaded at the same time. The third and fourth hayracks were used as a back-up, usually late in the evening for unloading the next morning when it was cool. We could usually bale faster in the field than the other guys could drive to the yard, unload, and drive back to the field.

One of us would toss bales from the hayrack into the barn. The other man or two inside the barn would carry the bales and stack them. Like stacking on the hayrack, the bales needed to criss-cross so they would interlock and not come tumbling down later on.

Urges by Gary Hennerberg

At some point the lower level of the barn would be filled making it impossible to unload from the trailer directly into the barn. Then we brought out the elevator with a constant loop that would bring up bales of hay, and once the elevator blades reached the top, they would flip over the metal and return back to the bottom. It was a constant loop, going over and over again. With the roaring gas engine and screeching of the blades, it was noisy. But it was also exhilarating. When we had enough help, there were two guys on the hayrack and two or three guys in the barn stacking. Of course, the guys on the hayrack had to pace the flow of bales. We didn't want to overload the guys in the hot barn.

By the end of summer, the barn usually became quite full. In a good year, when there was enough rain for the alfalfa to grow three or four crops, we could fill the barn to the rafters with hay. By fall, it was always satisfying to look into the barn and see that the year's crop had produced enough hay to easily feed all the cattle through winter.

❦

As I look back at the ritual of mowing, raking, baling, and stacking hay, it serves as quite the metaphor for searching, plucking, looking at and touching a pulled hair.

I seriously doubt that my hair pulling had anything to do with growing up on a farm and mowing, raking, and baling alfalfa. There are millions of people who pull their hair and they didn't all grow up on farms.

I don't think that it's the environment that causes a person to pull. I still believe, deep down, that trichotillomania is a condition a person is born with.

Trich is part of my complex fabric. I'm a hair puller. As a child, I could never have confronted it in this way or called it what it is. Rather, at that point in my life, I preferred to hide from it, but knew deep down inside that I enjoyed it. It raises my internal level of excitement and creates an unparalleled exhilaration. After more than 45 years of pulling, I haven't found anything that gives me a higher rush of euphoria.

The ritual goes on. My desire to pull loops on continually in a repetitive action that continues over and over and over and over again. I can't stop it. I'm powerless. But, oh, it feels so good.

> I still believe, deep down, that trichotillomania is a condition a person is born with.

CHAPTER 13
Perfection

My hair used to regrow back after I pulled it out. It gave me a second chance to leave it alone. Maybe even a third or fourth. But then it gave up. It stopped growing back once it knew I would just pull it out again.

At least that's what I think happened. How else to explain that I would pull it and it would grow back only to eventually stop.

Touching new incoming hair was exhilarating! Its texture was soft. In a few days it would grow out and feel like stubble. I would stroke it over and over again. But ultimately it would bother me. It had to go. Especially when I would look in a mirror and see the new growth was usually white. And as it would grow it would sometimes feel more coarse than my other hair. Its day would come and I'd have to pull it.

> My hair used to regrow back after I pulled it out. It gave me a second chance to leave it alone. Maybe even a third or fourth. But then it gave up.

Urges by Gary Hennerberg

So it wasn't too long before my scalp lost the appearance of open pores where regrowth could occur. The skin became smooth. Shiny. To this day when I touch my permanently damaged scalp, my fingertips effortlessly glide along.

I have some "holes" — bald spots — on the back of my head now. They're there to stay. The reason I pulled in those spots is because of the clips from years of wearing hairpieces. Every couple of years I'd buy a new hairpiece, and every couple of years it had to be made a little bigger to compensate for the area I would pull. For awhile, I used clips to secure my hair in back. But if the clips were too tight, they would irritate my scalp and sometimes a small welt would appear.

It was the welt from hitting my head when I was a small child that first aroused my sense of touch on my hair and scalp. And it was the welts from the hairpiece that even as an adult somehow got my attention and I pulled from there.

Those "holes" today are surrounded by hair. The hair is shaved but I'm embarrassed by how I look. But mercifully they are on the back of my head so I can't see them. I often touch the smooth skin of those "holes" and then feel my shaved hair around them. Sometimes I'll let my hair grow out for a couple of days without shaving. Then I'll run my fingers over the smooth "hole" and adjacent hair as a reminder of what I did to myself.

It's not a pleasant reminder. But it's my reality.

13 — Perfection

There were two things about farm life that I hated. One was chopping thistles in the late spring out of the pastures. And the other was cutting tall heads from the milo fields in the summer.

Those two jobs pretty much made for lousy summers at home from school. But even I have to admit a certain level of pride with how the pastures and fields looked once the jobs were done. There was a look of neatness and perfection that was highly satisfying for me. It was a sense of accomplishment.

By May of every spring, the thistles would grow just about anywhere you'd let them. They are obnoxious plants. And if you didn't tend to them, they could overtake valuable pasture, eventually crowding out and killing the good grasses that the cattle would live on every summer. They really did need to go.

Thistles have a single green stem with flat leaves. That said, I'd hardly call those prickly things that would grow on the sides leaves. They had needles. Sharp needles. You didn't dare put your hand on them. Thistles grew fast, seemingly overnight. And when they would mature, they would have a purple plume of seeds at the top. The purple seeds would turn to tan and the wind would carry the seeds all over. One thistle left to grow and mature in one growing season could yield literally dozens of new thistles the next year.

Urges by Gary Hennerberg

But because thistles could be so easily spread, if your neighbors didn't tend to their thistles, those nasty plants could turn up next year on your property. And believe me, there were plenty of neighbors from all directions who didn't tend to their thistles. That always perturbed Dad.

He was obsessed with thistles. Usually Dad would spray them in the pastures in the spring. We had a tank that would be mounted to the back of the small Ford tractor and he would drive back and forth, back and forth across the pastures to spray. He didn't like to do it because it was a seemingly needless cost. The spray would kill thistles and other undesired weeds. It was a good thing. But unfortunately, pastures being pastures, a fairly significant amount of the land in a pasture would be inaccessible with a tractor. There were always ravines, creeks and groves of trees surrounding the creeks. And occasionally there would be a "no man's land" surrounded by a ditch.

So you can guess who had the privilege of taking a spade to those ravines, creeks and no man's lands to chop thistles. My sister, Shirley, who is four years younger than I, wasn't much help. Yes, she would go out when forced to help, but I think she hated chopping thistles even more than I did. My youngest sister, Twila, was 13 years

13 — Perfection

younger than me so she probably had this privilege after I left home. Lucky her.

Sometimes Dad would help, but usually he was out doing more important things like getting the fields ready for planting. Mom rarely helped, but I know she did from time to time. She had other responsibilities to keep her busy.

So it was often me, by myself, toiling out in the pasture with my spade in tow. It was important to dig the thistle and its roots out of the soil. It wasn't enough to just cut off the purple head, or to cut it even with the ground. No, it had to be dug out so it wouldn't grow back in a few days. It was back breaking work.

> My hands were kept busy so the urge to pull my hair seemed to evaporate. So at one level, it seems I should have been glad to have been doing the work to take me away from hair pulling. But at another level, it took me away from what I'd rather have been doing, which is nothing and instead whiling away time yanking hair from my scalp. ⌒

But despite hating the job, when I finished a place that would have a lot of thistles in it, I would look back and be proud of how the pasture looked. springtime freshness of green grass

Urges by Gary Hennerberg

and leaves on the trees — there wasn't anything more calming. My hands were kept busy so the urge to pull my hair seemed to evaporate. So at one level, it seems I should have been glad to have been doing the work to take me away from hair pulling. But at another level, it took me away from what I'd rather have been doing, which is nothing and instead whiling away time yanking hair from my scalp.

Thankfully, thistle season only lasted during the late spring, May and June mostly.

But by August, another dreaded job would begin: chopping tall heads out of the milo fields. Chopping tall heads may have been worse than chopping thistles, actually.

First I should describe a "tall head." A tall head is a stalk of milo that grows a foot or more higher than the rest of the milo heads. Milo, or sorghum as some call it, is a crop raised for its grain to feed livestock. Humans don't consume it. We needed the milo crop every fall harvest to feed to the cattle during the coming winter months when they couldn't graze in the pastures (those same pastures where I had chopped the thistles).

Milo is planted in the spring, usually in May. It is planted in rows, about 30 inches apart. A seed is planted every few inches in its row, so it grows close together. At first it looks like a green corn plant, but by summer heads

13 — Perfection

of grain emerge. Each plant's head of grain has dozens, perhaps hundreds, of individual milo pellets. They're small. Perhaps one eighth of an inch in diameter. And as they mature, they turn a reddish brown.

We would plant over 100 acres of milo. That was a lot back in those days, but not so much for large farmers today.

Back then, Dad would use fertilizer for the plants to grow up strong and healthy and herbicides to kill the weeds. He would carefully drive the tractor through the fields to cultivate the milo field and take out weeds. Sometimes the weeds would grow thicker in certain parts of the field. Then he would mount the sprayer on back of the tractor to spray them.

But there was no spray that would eradicate a tall head.

The grain of a tall head was probably just fine for the cattle to eat, but Dad wanted them chopped out for a couple of reasons. First, because it was his belief that when he would harvest the milo in the fall that a single tall head would knock out several perfectly good heads from going into the combine. He was probably right, but I think it was more rationalization for the second reason: he wanted the field to appear perfect.

So we would walk the fields, chopping out the tall heads. Fortunately, tall heads didn't have to be dug out

Urges by Gary Hennerberg

of the soil. But we would zig zag through a field for hours chopping out every stray head.

August was usually a very hot month with temperatures easily into the 90s, often over 100 degrees in the afternoon. So we would chop the tall heads in the morning, then perhaps again in the evening.

In the spring of 1968, when I was 11, Dad bought a farm close by. He was so proud of that farm because several acres of land were on a flat river bottom with rows that would extend a half mile. The rows could be long and straight. The rich soil of the river bottom meant the yield per acre of grain should be higher than that of the hillside fields.

He bought the farm during the winter months so he hadn't had a chance to see the fields during the summer. The far end of the field, a half mile away, could only be accessed and seen by the previous landowner and the owner of the neighboring farm. It was fairly remote.

So knowing my Dad's obsession with having the perfect field, imagine our dismay the first year that river bottom field was planted in milo to discover that the far end of the field was infested with black cane.

Let me tell you about black cane. This was an obnoxious plant. Worse than thistles. Much worse.

It could grow to tower 6 feet tall, fully 3 feet higher than a milo plant. The stalk was thin and the grain was

13 — Perfection

black. And it would take over a field, completely crowding out the milo we intended to harvest. This was not a good development.

The day Dad and I walked through the field and approached the far south end, a half mile away, I knew we were in trouble that year.

There were acres of black cane. There was nothing that could be sprayed on it to kill it.

Instead of chopping it off, like we did the tall heads, we pulled black cane out of the sandy soil. If digging out thistles was back breaking, this was back breaking times ten.

We would go down one single row, bend over and pull, move six inches. Bend over and pull, move six inches. This would go on for perhaps 200 feet per row. And there were dozens and dozens of rows where the black cane infestation was so bad.

This would be a project that would take days to complete. Day after hot August day, we would return to the river bottom to pull black cane.

After a week we had made progress moving from one side of the field to another. It had rained in the meantime, giving the vegetation much needed water. So Dad decided to walk over to the rows where we had pulled several days earlier. He couldn't believe his eyes. The black cane we had worked so hard to pull, which we threw down

Urges by Gary Hennerberg

between the rows of milo, had re-rooted and started to grow again! The stalks that had been lying on their side had literally turned back up toward the sky and were growing.

> The black cane we had worked so hard to pull, which we threw down between the rows of milo, had re-rooted and started to grow again!

This was not a happy discovery. Now we had to add a step to the process. We would pull the black cane, shake the soil from the roots, and then cut the roots from the stalk. Oh, brother. It made back breaking work times ten, now about times thirty.

So we started all over again, back where we started.

I thought that summer would never end. Why couldn't we just let this go this year and next year plant a different crop in the field so it could be managed? No, that wouldn't do. We had to pull, shake and chop off the roots for what had to be a zillion stalks of black cane.

But the next summer Dad did plant the field to wheat and after a couple of years he was able to plant milo and corn in this field. It would eventually be the proud field he dreamed it would be: half mile rows on a river bottom that was picture perfect.

13 — Perfection

My hair didn't grow back after a few years of having pulled it out. I suppose my hair and black cane had something in common in a bizarre kind of way.

For the longest time, I could pull hair and it would grow back. But then slowly I realized that the hair that had grown back, and that I had pulled out a second or third time, wasn't coming back in.

My hair gave up. I had succeeded in my own version of chopping out the obnoxious. And upon the realization of what I had done to my head of hair — that it would no longer grow back after years of pulling it out — I cried. And I cried. The tears streamed down my face for days, out of sight from everyone. I cried when I was alone, because there was no one — no one who could possibly identify with these mysterious urges.

> Upon the realization of what I had done to my head of hair — that it would no longer grow back after years of pulling it out — I cried. And I cried. The tears streamed down my face for days, out of sight from everyone.

CHAPTER 14

Grooming

I've been obsessed with looking good for much of my life. What a dichotomy. What an inconsistency. I want to look good. Make that perfect. But I pull out my hair. Now exactly what can that do to advance good looks?

So maybe my obsession for perfection came from my Dad when we had to make the pastures and fields look perfect. I doubt it.

Maybe that obsession comes from wanting to keep my hair pulling a secret. If my hair was combed perfectly, you wouldn't see the bald spots. As I look back at pictures of myself as a child, I can see that I did a pretty good job of mastering the right angles of the right comb-over.

But I think it's deeper than any of that. I think I have a "perfection gene" but with a wire crossed. It drives me to think that pulling my hair out contributes to

> As I look back at pictures of myself as a child, I can see that I did a pretty good job of mastering the right angles of the right comb-over.

Urges by Gary Hennerberg

my perfection. Perhaps that gives new meaning to the term "haywire."

If my hair has to be perfect, then my clothes have to be perfect, too. After all, if every hair is in its place and my clothes are clean, pressed, and most importantly, have fashion sense, my perfectly combed hair looks natural, right? Having every hair in place but wearing disheveled clothes would be in inconsistency. People would look at me and see that something was amiss. I couldn't have that.

Mercifully, God gave me the perfection gene to compliment my hair pulling gene. I could pull and pull to my heart's delight and cover it up, dress immaculately, and fool everyone. Or so I thought.

> I think I have a "perfection gene" but with a wire crossed. It drives me to think that pulling my hair out contributes to my perfection.

My life is that of irony. And I have the plaque to prove it. It happened in 1970. In addition to projects like dairy, 4-H offered other programs as well. I'm uncertain where this one belonged under the head, heart, hands, and health philosophy of 4-H, but there was an annual competition category at County Club Days called Best Groomed Boy.

14 — Grooming

I was in the eighth grade, toward the end of my childhood run of being in 4-H. The Best Groomed Boy competition was an opportunity for boys of all ages to dress their best, make sure our hair was combed properly and to see, I suppose, if us farm boys could clean up for a day. I don't think most farm boys ever considered dressing well to be a priority. But I always wanted to be well-dressed, even if I wasn't sure how to do it. Watching TV in the 1960s, where it seemed every man who lived in the city constantly wore a coat and tie, influenced my perception of how a guy should look. I decided early on in my life that I, too, wanted to wear a coat and tie to work. I believed it meant that you had achieved a certain status in life. And besides, men and women look better when we are dressed to the nines.

My folks bought my first coat and tie, at least my first dressy outfit as a teenager, in about March of 1970. I really don't recall where we bought this coat and tie. It was probably in Lincoln where it seemed we always went when we needed to buy something special. The smaller towns just didn't have much to choose from.

I guess there were a couple of reasons to buy this suit. I needed a suit, for one thing. There was the Best Groomed Boy contest. And probably the most pressing reason was the fact that I was in Confirmation classes. Confirmation was a two year study program at the

Urges by Gary Hennerberg

Lutheran Church where kids in the 7th and 8th grade would meet frequently with a pastor for Bible study and discussion. The last year of my Confirmation class, when I was an 8th grader, was held at the Lutheran Church in Hanover. The classes in Hanover brought together kids from three or four churches in the area. Since I would be going to Hanover High School starting in the fall of 1970, it was a way to meet a few of the kids I would later go to high school with.

    I didn't study the Bible very well. If I wasn't in school, I was at home doing chores, not leaving a lot of free time for reading. And as an adult I still don't read the Bible like I should even though I enjoy reading. But something tells me that most of us when we're age 13 and 14 didn't pay a lot of attention to such endeavors, although certainly there had to be something we took away from those Saturday morning classes. I didn't mind going to Confirmation classes because it meant those Saturday mornings I didn't have to work at home on the farm.

    At the end of the Confirmation course, in the spring of 1970, we had to take a test. If we passed, we were confirmed. Of course, almost everyone passed. They probably passed almost every teenager to spare us from having a negative church experience, but I didn't know that at the time.

14 — Grooming

The Confirmation ceremony at our church was in May of 1970. There were just two of us that would be confirmed. Bruce was a distant relative, but more of a childhood friend. His Mom and Dad, Gilbert and Carolyn, and my Mom and Dad were best of friends. They remained lifelong friends until one very sad day in June of 2009 when Gilbert and Carolyn died together in an automobile accident. They lived on the Nebraska side of the state line road, so Bruce went to school in Nebraska schools. As we got older and became teenagers, each going to different schools in different states, we drifted apart.

But I digress. I'll never forget the suit coat. And the complementing slacks and tie. The colors were green. A 70s thing I guess. The jacket was plaid and to this day I remember it as being a good looking garment. It was vibrant and fresh. I still have the pictures from Confirmation. In color!

I'm not sure why I wanted to enter the Best Groomed Boy contest that March. It was my last year in 4-H and perhaps I saw it as a rite of passage.

There were always several boys in the competition, and I knew the odds of me receiving top honors weren't very good. There were a lot better looking boys than me who were thinner. And deep down inside, I knew I had bald spots to cover.

Urges by Gary Hennerberg

Yet by 1970 I had let my hair grow out longer so I had more hair to cover the bald spots. Even as I look at those pictures today, it's not obvious that I had bald spots, yet I know they were there. Perhaps by the time I became a teen-ager I became more adept at covering them.

The contest was in Washington at the high school like all past County Club Days. I had taken special care that morning to make sure my hair had been washed and combed just so. My clothes were clean and pressed. I shined my shoes, and I made sure my belt was properly aligned with my pants and shirt. And the tie was a clip-on, so all I had to do was make sure it was clipped-on straight.

Mom drove me to Washington for the event. We arrived at the high school, went inside, and found the room where were to gather.

The judging for this contest was rather strange, as I recall. All the boys in the competition — probably around ten of us — stood in a line. When asked to step to the middle of the stage we did. When asked to turn around, we did. That was about it.

I don't recall the announcement and how that happened. Perhaps I was too stunned to realize that not only did I get a Blue Ribbon, but I was named Washington County's Best Groomed Boy for 1970.

14 — Grooming

I still have the plaque to prove it. The plaque symbolized for me that I could overcome the odds of looking bad from years of hair pulling.

I was so proud of that honor. It was a boost in my confidence that maybe this chubby kid with a hair-pulling problem could make it through life without the scars showing. That maybe someday I would stop pulling my hair and be normal, like all the other kids. And that I'd be handsome enough to pursue my childhood dream of being Steve Hart.

Sometimes I wonder if the judge knew my little secret and was being especially charitable. Perhaps it was a boost to help my self-esteem. I'll never know. But what happened that day was a gift for a teenager who deep down inside was doing my best to hide my shame of being a hair-puller. Something so hideous, so bad, that I had to be the only kid in the entire world who would do such a bizarre thing.

Urges by Gary Hennerberg

I went on to represent Washington County at the Kansas State Fair to compete in the state contest. There must have been nearly 100 boys in that competition.

I didn't win. I don't even recall how I placed. But it didn't matter. My self-esteem had been lifted.

As an adult, I've questioned the value of contests and sporting events for our kids. Sometimes it seems like a lot of unnecessary pressure. Or rewarding them when a reward wasn't earned.

But I've softened my stance on that as I've written chapters like this one about winning the Best Groomed Boy contest, delivering a Project Talk, or showing Whimpie at the County Fair.

These were all very meaningful events in my life. They gave me confidence at a time when I needed building up. They gave my self-esteem a boost when at times all I would do is wallow in self-pity, shame and despair. The compulsion to pull my hair was consuming. But to the casual acquaintance, friend or well-meaning relative, they couldn't have known my anguish. Deep down inside I struggled with my urges daily.

And therein lies my compassion for people. There are those people whose urges can be observed. But there are so many people, I sense, who keep their urges private. Like me, they think of their compulsion or obsession as so bizarre that they don't seek help and don't know where to turn.

It's my hope that we can support each other better. That we can sense when a child needs a little extra "TLC." And as we look around, recognize that many of us have our own issue or urge, and are doing our best to hide it and control it.

CHAPTER 15
Horns

Hiding my hair-pulling urges while at school was difficult.

But I only thought I hid my pulling. I think people have something of a sixth sense about others. We sense when someone is hiding something. We sense if they truly mean what they say.

Sometimes we let our intuition kick in and listen to what our consciousness is telling us. Sometimes we ignore it.

I pulled my hair at school. I can remember some particularly bad days when I would look down at the floor and see hair all over. My heart would sink. And I'd hope that no one noticed it. Sure.

My frenzies would go wild. As a youngster, I would twist and turn several strands of hair together. Ultimately I would somehow wad them together so there would be a small knot on the

> To this day, even with a shaved head, I can still feel the sensation and hear the sound of hair pulling. One strand out. Then another. And another. All in slow motion.

Urges by Gary Hennerberg

ends of my hair. That made for great pulling. I would twist and turn my hair for several seconds, get a knot made and in one tug I could pull out perhaps a half dozen or even a dozen strands of hair. As I would pull the knotted group, to this day, even with a shaved head, I can still feel the sensation and hear the sound of hair pulling. One strand out. Then another. And another. All in slow motion. Time would slow down as I pulled my hair and an instant could seem like several seconds. It was euphoric!

But by the end of the day, when I'd look down on the hardwood floor of my grade school classroom, I would see dozens of groups of knotted hair on the floor in disarray.

I was so powerless. I didn't want to pull my hair. But I still did it. That makes no sense, does it? How could the urge and desire to pull so outweigh the reality of hair lying on the floor? And a bald spot getting bigger by the day. Or even by the minute.

Life isn't easy for kids. It should be the most wonderful time of our lives. As kids, we stress over things within our world. As adults, we often discount their stresses, thinking our stress in the adult world — finances, careers, family — somehow trump the stress kids feel.

That's wrong. Our perceptions are our realities no matter our age.

15 — Horns

The grade school in Hollenberg, where I attended grades 1 through 8, had two classrooms. One classroom was for First through Fourth Grade, and another was for Fifth through Eighth Grade. Every year there were either four or five kids in my class.

During my First Grade, and perhaps Second Grade too, there was still a High School in the same building. But in the 1960s consolidation of rural public schools closed what there was of Hollenberg High School. After completing eighth grade, the next year would mean going to Hanover High School, about 15 miles down a twisting and turning road along the Little Blue River.

I was terrified knowing that someday I would have to go to Hanover High School. I didn't want to go to Hanover. I'm not sure where I wanted to go. We lived in a far corner of the school boundary, named Unified School District 223.

Another high school was in the county seat, Washington, where so many of my 4-H experiences with County Club Days had been held. We were 15 miles from Washington, about the same distance as to Hanover. But the road to Washington was paved most of the distance and had fewer curves.

Across the state line, in Nebraska, the town of Diller had a high school. It was smaller than Hanover, but it was about the closest of them all, perhaps 10 miles away.

Urges by Gary Hennerberg

Then there was Fairbury, also in Nebraska, about 17 miles away.

But it's not like there were choices. Or if there were choices, I don't think my folks explored them. We were in the Hanover district and that would be where I'd go. And I wasn't happy about it.

The stresses of worrying about high school took their toll on me. I would suddenly go from my class of five of us to a class of around 48. That was a huge jump, silly as that may sound to someone living in a large urban area.

One of the biggest changes, too, would be taking a very long bus ride. The route to Hollenberg Grade School for those first eight years was relatively short. I was the first to be picked up, the last to be left off, and the total trip probably took close to 30 minutes.

Going to Hanover meant I was still the first on the route, but with all the stops at various farmsteads it took an hour to get to school, and an hour to get home. It was a big bus. It could hold up to 48 of us. Our bus driver was a friendly fellow named Art. He smiled and greeted me with a good morning and good bye every day. I liked him. As a Freshman I sat toward the front of the bus. By the time I was a Senior I would sit in the back, where the upperclassmen would sit.

It was two hours every day in an uncomfortable school bus that bounced over rough country gravel

15 — Horns

roads. And the bus ride gave me plenty of time to stew about the day. In the mornings, as we would stop at farm after farm, the bus would get fuller and fuller. It made me anxious. By the time we'd arrive at school, the bus would be completely full.

At the end of the day, the bus would start completely full and slowly empty until I was the last kid on the bus.

I was always taller than most everyone my same age while growing up. That physical attribute served me well to hide my hair pulling from kids I went to school with.

Remarkably, I don't recall ever being harassed by other kids about being a hair puller. Perhaps it was because I was bigger than most. Maybe it's because I avoided any situation that would have put me in a position to reveal anything. I kept my head down, so to speak. Oh, there was one bully in high school who was a couple of years older than me who would harass me. It was, looking back, low level stuff, but it still bothered me a lot. He never hit me. It was verbal abuse. I got off light, even if it didn't seem like it at the time. But I was relieved when he graduated. That gave me a couple of years of a hassle-free existence.

I'll never forget the day when some classmates couldn't help but have a literal birds-eye view of the top of my head.

Urges by Gary Hennerberg

It was when I was a senior in high school. The bleachers in our high school had wheels under them and would collapse when pushed together to free up space on the gym floor.

One day there was to be an assembly of some type and I was standing on the floor. Some of my classmates were sitting on the top row of the bleachers, which had been collapsed inward. They really weren't supposed to be sitting up there, but hey, we were teenagers.

> "Hey, Gary has horns!"

As I stood below, I'll always hear the words from a classmate when he said something loud enough for me and lots of kids nearby to hear that sent me chills.

"Hey, Gary has horns!"

If I could have pushed a button to make myself invisible, I would have been frantically looking for it.

But something amazing happened. At least now looking back it was notable.

No one seemed to care.

The guys were just teenagers being teenagers. Perhaps there was enough maturity from these 17 year olds to just let it go and not hassle me.

I never heard another word about my horns again. Mercifully, they apparently didn't care.

15 — Horns

As I write this, well over 30 years later, I realize that perhaps God was sending me a message that day. A message that says I shouldn't have been obsessed with what people around me thought. Sure, my classmate saw my "holes" and dubbed them "horns". But no one else chimed in. Maybe there was a feeling of compassion from a few of the kids in my class. I doubt it was ever a secret that I had bald spots. And I'm sure that some of them observed me pulling my hair.

> I realize that perhaps God was sending me a message that day

Maybe they felt pity on me and I never knew it. I think that adults, and mature teenagers, can actually have a soft spot and pause long enough to realize that they, too, have their own issues or urges.

That's the good news if you're an adult.

But what about those years as a teenager. I think middle school age — those in the 12 to 15 year old phase — tend to be much meaner and judgmental towards others than at any other age. Especially now.

I was once that age, too, and during those years I pulled my hair. I don't recall being hassled much, but we lived in a small community and times were much different.

Urges by Gary Hennerberg

There were mean kids then and perhaps more so today. But something tells me that human nature hasn't changed that much. Call me an optimist, and perhaps not always realistic, but I think there are more kids who feel empathy toward others than there are kids who sit back and judge them and make fun of them. Or at least that's what I prefer to hope.

Chapter 16
Amputation

The pulling frenzies continued into high school. Surely, I thought, as I would get older this urge would leave me. But it didn't. I kept thinking there must be a way to rid myself of this bizarre behavior.

Sometimes I thought that cutting off my left arm or my left hand would make the urge to pull go away.

I've always pulled only with my left hand. Even though I'm right handed, it's awkward to pull with my right hand. Yes, I've tried pulling with my right hand, but in addition to the awkwardness, I was never drawn into my euphoric trance stage as when I pulled with my left hand.

> Sometimes I thought that cutting off my left arm or my left hand would make the urge to pull go away.

This should be logical, really. But there is no logic with such illogical behavior.

As a child and teenager, I was convinced I was the only person on this planet who pulled my hair. I knew I did it. But I couldn't admit it to anyone, or talk about it with anyone. So I relied on talking to myself. A lot. And I hoped that somehow

Urges by Gary Hennerberg

I would find the strength and source to answer my own questions.

༺༻

High school is a time of discovery, but in a different kind of way than that of being in grade or elementary school.

I think most of us by our teen years start to look for clues about what we will become as adults. What will our personality be like? What will we do? How will we survive in this mean, harsh world? But most of all, I suppose we promise ourselves that we'll never be like our parents.

Early in my life, I knew I didn't have the heart to be a farmer like my Dad. And I knew that it would disappoint him greatly when the time would come to tell him. So in my mind I knew I had to discover a talent I could use in my life to more than compensate for that loss in his life.

One of my discoveries of talent was when I gave my Project Talk about my dairy project. By the time I got to high school, I was able to pursue speaking and making presentations. I loved theater and speech classes and acting in school plays. Every winter and spring there were speech tournaments with a variety of categories, including one-act plays, reading poetry, extemporaneous speaking, dramatic interpretation and more. I probably tried all of these categories at one time or another during my high school years. But by the time I was a Junior or

16 — Amputation

Senior, I started to do fairly well earning good scores and ratings in contests.

During one of those last two years of high school, our teacher, Mr. J., encouraged me to create a dramatic interpretation from the book *All Quiet on the Western Front*.

This is a book written about a soldier's life during World War I in Europe. It's a dark story. I can't imagine that there were times when people had to endure the physical and mental hardships of such a difficult war.

This is not an uplifting story. Rather, it's more a documentation of men losing their lives and limbs to war.

My dramatic interpretation, as I recall, was drawn from a part of the book where the author has been wounded in war and lays in a hospital recovering. I took some license to write my dramatic interpretation of this scene.

The interpretation I drew upon was that this soldier begins to hallucinate about what has happened, how he misses his mother, who is dying of cancer, and his father who works around the clock in a meaningless job.

At one point, the soldier senses that he has lost his legs. And then he realizes that he has lost his arms. He lays in a bed crying out for help but no one is listening to him. No one is helping him. He has no where to go. And he's left there to die.

Urges by Gary Hennerberg

At the first tournament I stood in front of the judge giving this eight-or-so-minute dramatic interpretation. As I gave my interpretation, I naturally moved my body and gestured with my arms and hands. I scored very well doing it this way.

The judge made a suggestion that had never occurred to me. He thought it could be even more powerful if I were to sit on a chair, with my arms to my side, instead of standing. By keeping my arms and legs perfectly still, it would visually heighten the effect of the soldier having lost his arms and legs for the audience, and it would challenge me to deliver my dramatic interpretation without arm, leg and body movement. Everything about this interpretation would be delivered using only my voice and facial expression.

I rehearsed it with Mr. J. the following Monday, just as the judge had suggested.

The change made an amazing change to my dramatic interpretation. It altered the entire delivery and drama of the moment. It was intense. It was exhausting. And it was a change I kept for the rest of that season as I scored well during the remaining tournaments of the school year.

But there may have been an even greater message that came through to me. Here was a judge at a tournament who made a suggestion and I tried it.

16 — Amputation

It was a powerful message where for a few moments on stage I could dramatize the sensation of not having any arms. It meant I couldn't have pulled my hair. My curiosity of going through life without arms, and without the ability to pull my hair could be vicariously experienced in a dramatic interpretation that would settle that crazy dream once and for all: I'd rather pull my hair than go through life without arms.

> My curiosity of going through life without arms, and without the ability to pull my hair could be vicariously experienced in a dramatic interpretation that would settle that crazy dream once and for all: I'd rather pull my hair than go through life without arms.

Somewhere in this world is a teacher who was generously giving his time judging high school kids on a Saturday morning who inspired me to do something different with a dramatic interpretation. It was a change intended only for the tournament stage. But little did he know it would change my outlook on the stage on which I stand in my life.

Urges by Gary Hennerberg

I still have momentary thoughts about life without my left arm. But thankfully, logic prevails and I go on.

Yes, not having a left arm would have probably allowed me to have had a full head of hair. Of course, it would never have been worth it.

I would think about strapping my arm to my side. But it was never practical. I would put gloves on my hands but take them off in an instant.

I've never forgotten my dramatic interpretation of this young man in World War I who lived without his arms and legs. While delivering the dramatic interpretation sitting perfectly without moving my arms still never stopped me from pulling my hair, it gave me comfort knowing that an alternative wasn't better.

Chapter 17
Blame

Surely there is someone or something I can blame. That would be an easy out for me, wouldn't it? Just transfer the responsibility elsewhere.

But I can't say for sure that I've ever blamed anyone for my plight.

I could have blamed Bill. He's the one who hit the rut in the field which caused me to bump my head. Then a welt appeared on my head and prompted my curiosity to touch my scalp. That sequence of events lead me to pull my hair for the rest of my life. But I never blamed Bill.

I could have blamed my Dad, for no particular reason. Like most fathers, he had to enforce some level of discipline with a son.

I can recall some days when I'd blame stress.

I can recall some days when I'd blame stress. Other days I'd blame God. Mostly I just wanted an explanation. I want to know less about "why me" and more about what the reason is that I harbor this urge.

Urges by Gary Hennerberg

Other days I'd blame God.

Mostly I just wanted an explanation. I want to know less about "why me" and more about what the reason is that I harbor this urge. This isn't natural.

The fact is that I can't blame this disorder on someone or something. But after years of struggle with accepting myself as who I am, I came to a realization much later in my life:

For most of my life, and especially during my childhood, I have blamed myself.

I was an adult before I discovered that there was a name for this disorder. Trichotillomania is a term coined by a French dermatologist in 1889 to describe the compulsive or irresistible urge he saw in patients to pluck out their hair. The word trichotillomania is derived from the Greek thrix, hair; tillein, to pull; and mania, madness or frenzy. The name "trichotillomania" is disturbing to me because it suggests I'm crazy. I'm not. That's why those

> The name "trichotillomania" is disturbing to me because it suggests I'm crazy. I'm not. That's why those of us who pull often use the word "trich" — pronounced "trick" — or abbreviate it to TTM.

17 — Blame

of us who pull often use the word "trich" — pronounced "trick" — or abbreviate it to TTM.

I learned over the years, too, that there are other people in this world with this behavior. And I learned of an organization for people like me who pull our hair, named the Trichotillomania Learning Center. It's a small organization started in 1991 by Christina Pearson. I've come to know and adore Christina over the years. Christina wrote the beautiful Foreword for this book. I'm convinced God sent her to this earth to start this organization. The organization's name conveniently abbreviates to TLC, because most of us need some tender loving care after years of shame and isolation.

Trich has probably been around as long as there have been people with hair. Trich was considered to be a rare disorder in the past because people seldom sought help. And to this day, many doctors fail to give a proper diagnosis because they haven't been trained to screen for or recognize this disorder.

But trich is more common than first thought. It seems women outnumber men as hair pullers, perhaps as much as 10-to-1. That makes me a minority within a group who has an already obscure disorder. Epidemiological studies indicate that compulsive hair pulling affects some 2–4% of the population. It is estimated that in the United States

Urges by Gary Hennerberg

alone there are as many as 10 million people who struggle with trich.

On the surface, it seems 2% is a big number. Imagine yourself in a room with 1,000 randomly chosen people only to discover that up to 20 of us have trich. That doesn't seem plausible, does it? You don't look around and see 20 people with unusual bald spots, do you?

Of course you don't see us. Some hair pullers whom I have met over the years live in isolation and rarely go out in public because they don't want to be seen. Other hair pullers are experts at hiding bald spots. We spend considerable time in front of a mirror masking our self-inflicted damage. Many of us have worn hairpieces or wigs. Sometimes we wear caps and hats. Women will apply make-up, eyebrow liner and false eyelashes to hide eyebrow and eyelash pulling. I've gone to many conferences over the years attended by people with trich, and as I look at most of the people there, I wouldn't know they are hair pullers.

We're just that good at hiding it.

The amount of scientific research about trichotillomania grows every year. There are several books and reports that address this subject.

But there is no known cure as I write this. No magic pills that will make you stop. There are medications that have been documented to help ease the urge, and

17 — Blame

perhaps for some people it works. I personally haven't tried any medications. The conversations I have had with a handful of people who have tried them suggest that medications aren't the answer and often yield undesirable side effects.

Counseling is an option that may help in managing the urges. I went to a psychiatrist many years ago. He was familiar with trich and had many good suggestions for me. But after a few sessions I realized that I wasn't listening to what he recommended. My urge to pull was far greater than my urge to stop. Strangely, while I wanted to stop I wasn't ready to leave my comfort zone. How bizarre that pulling my hair would put me in a comfort zone I wouldn't want to leave.

> My urge to pull was far greater than my urge to stop. Strangely, while I wanted to stop I wasn't ready to leave my comfort zone. How bizarre that pulling my hair would put me in a comfort zone I wouldn't want to leave.

I wonder if the counseling would have been more successful if instead of giving me coping exercises and behavior modification, we could have explored self-acceptance. In other words, if I was adamant about pulling yet wouldn't stop, giving me coping mechanisms to help me understand why I do it, and help me learn how to accept and live with it, may have been more helpful.

I have wondered if there was a food that I've loved that contributed to the manifestation of the urge to pull hair. Was it the strawberries that my Grandmother grew in her garden that I would gorge on every summer? Or the yeast in her homemade bread that I so loved?

I doubt it.

I've tried hypnosis and I stopped pulling for about six months. It was such a relief while it lasted, but when life started to get stressed I "fell off the wagon."

My notes from back in 1999, when I first tried hypnosis, and from early 2000, when I started pulling again, are comforting even to this day.

4/6/99 — My first hypnosis experience. James (the hypnotist) told me "You're in control," "You're in charge." That's how I first stopped.

6/8/99 — Crossed away from the urges at that point. That night, during the hypnosis, I don't recall the message, but I recall this: A sudden flash of light and the sensation that God had taken the trich away. I was free! He took it back! He took it back!

But I started pulling again a few months later. I've wondered if God gave it back. But I don't think it works that way with God. I prayed about it. But in praying, I realize that trich is "sewn in" to my fabric, never to be taken away. It's in my DNA. It's for me to accept and manage just as someone with borderline type 2 diabetes might, for example, be able to manage their condition through diet and exercise.

> I realize that trich is "sewn in" to my fabric, never to be taken away. It's in my DNA. It's for me to accept and manage.

1/22/00 — Today I went through the tunnel to the Pyramids. I went into my own pyramid, and under it I saw my own room. Inside was a figure that I would first throw to the ground and break into pieces. It represented the bad in my life. The good were all in drawers inside the room. They were always there for me, I just didn't know it. I can draw from my strength by opening any of those drawers at any time.

Several days later I tried hypnosis again.

1/30/00 — Tonight I will have a healing dream. Went through the tunnel to a lake. I arrived at the side which was cloudy, windy, turbulent. I got on a boat and crossed the water into calm waters, where it was sunny. Upon getting to shore, I laid in the sun where I was able to allow all of the positive influences into my life, and leave behind the bad. I could heal. Tonight would be a healing dream.

These notes from hypnosis sessions are encouraging. So full of hope. But I couldn't break the spell of hair pulling.

Urges by Gary Hennerberg

I would later learn that other people with trichotillomania had tried hypnotherapy and had similar results. They, like me, would stop for awhile only to resume again.

I've tried biofeedback, too, with no change in behavior.

A positive development has come from a study of a common dietary supplement named N-Acetylcysteine. It's an amino acid supplement found at nutrition and health food stores. Early results indicate that taking this supplement may help reduce hair pulling urges for some people.

I've tried other forms of alternate therapy as well. I haven't found a cure, but I want to believe there is something out there, yet to be discovered, that will isolate the cause of trich and will give me and all other hair pullers the tools to help manage it, or even better, eradicate it.

Meeting other hair pullers is an experience like no other. You see, when I met other pullers the thing that stuck me most is this: first, usually there is no obvious sign that they pull their hair. No bald spots are evident. The hair might be combed a bit unusually, but that's it. They may be wearing a hat or cap. Next, I observed that they are, well, so normal. They're not weird. These are people you would meet in your neighborhood grocery store or at a school function. And finally, what I have observed

17 — Blame

is that hair pullers are intelligent people. Articulate. Well read. Friendly.

The Trichotillomania Learning Center sponsors several events each year that allows hair pullers to meet each other and hear presentations from medical and psychiatric professionals, counselors, and other hair pullers. The first time I met other hair pullers was at a TLC retreat in 1996. The retreats are one time a year, usually at a remote conference center, usually a place with cabins and camping. It's very serene and calming. Hair pullers and professionals from around the world attend. It's an opportunity to meet others, interact, and discover more about yourself and this compulsion that can consume you.

Since trich seems to affect women more than men, there were only a few guys present at the retreat while there were hundreds of women there. But everyone gets along well. I remember at my first retreat that there were multiple sessions that we could choose from to attend. The speakers were mostly medical professionals and counselors. I vividly recall some of the presentations and how they touched me. Many of us found ourselves in deep thought and concentration. Tears flowed, but amongst fellow hair pullers, it didn't matter. There was no shame in crying for we all knew what brought us to this point and this place.

Urges by Gary Hennerberg

In 2007 I attended one of TLC's weekend conferences in Washington, D.C. This event is more formal than the retreat in that the conference is at a hotel and sessions are in meeting rooms. In the more than ten years since I had attended a retreat or conference, the composition of the attendees had changed. In the 1990s there were only a few teenagers who attended. Now there were dozens of teens and their parents, some traveling from outside the U.S., in addition to mostly women and a few men who were hair pullers.

During this conference, I encountered a young girl, probably around 20 years old, who resembled one of my daughters. She was tall, brunette, and very pretty. At one point while walking between sessions I remarked to her that she looked just like my daughter. I would never have guessed that she pulled her hair. Yes, I could see that her hair was styled and combed somewhat out of the ordinary, but the casual observer would never have guessed that she was a hair puller.

Later that day we were in a session together. It was a session led by Joan Kaylor, one of the counselors (who graciously donate their time to these events). Joan led us through an hour-long exercise of deep concentration and visualization. It's difficult to describe what she took us through, but as the session went on it became more and more emotionally intense. It isn't unusual during these

17 — Blame

conferences to see someone burst into tears. In fact, every room has a box of tissues and it often is passed around the room. In the session that day, this young girl who looked like my daughter burst into tears and suddenly bolted and left the room. It broke my heart. Someone went after her to check on her. While she didn't return to that session, I did see her later on. The thoughts that brought her to tears are her private experiences, but for most of us it is healthy to release some of the shame and guilt that has accumulated for our entire lives.

There isn't a lot of "evidence" to be found for why we pull. There are theories advanced by leading medical and psychiatric practitioners. I'd say that everyone who has trichotillomania and who I've spoken with knows deep-down that the theories are mostly right.

There is, for example, the notion that we are wired differently. With only a few brain scans as evidence, the medical community is seeing that those of us with trich have evidence of different brain composition. I could have told them that without a brain scan, as could virtually every other person I've talked to who counts trich as part of their lives. But we live in a world where people demand scientific evidence. And this evidence doesn't come at any small expense.

There are also studies suggesting trich is genetic and family studies are in process.

Urges by Gary Hennerberg

So who is there to fund this work? Those of us with trich could band together and each make a monetary contribution. Some of us do, but the fact is that the amount of money needed is way beyond the everyday gift most of us can give. Even joining together, our money can only do so much. Thankfully, there are grants from the National Institute of Mental Health that started research in about 2006.

There may be incentive for big pharmaceutical companies to fund such studies and then develop a medication to help us. It will take years of research and development and enormous investment for any corporation to rationalize a reason to support these efforts. After all, trich isn't life-threatening, is it?

Maybe. Maybe not. I can still hear Christina Pearson relay a story that put the terms "life-threatening" and "trichotillomania" in the same sentence.

She invited me to a small reception at the 2007 TLC conference in Washington, D.C. When the subject of trich as a life-threatening disorder came up, she relayed a phone conversation she had with the parents of a teenager who had trich. Christina's story goes something like this:

"Don't tell me that trich isn't life threatening. And don't tell that to the parents of an 18-year-old girl who, after years and years of pulling, enormous shame and anxiety, decided

17 — Blame

> "Don't tell me that trich isn't life threatening. And don't tell that to the parents of an 18-year-old girl who, after years and years of pulling, enormous shame and anxiety, decided she couldn't cope anymore and put a gun to her head to end her life."

My eyes welled up with tears when she said that. Like many teens, the thought of suicide entered my mind. There is a point where you decide you can't take the urge to pull any longer. That the shame is too much to bear. That maybe life on this earth isn't worth the snickering from other kids. Or that you feel worthless and have no future in your life.

With the repetitive nature of trich, when you pull your hair over and over and over again, if the repetitive thought of ending your life pervades you and you think about killing yourself over and over and over again … oh, this sentence makes me weary. For I pray that there is no teenager or adult who ever takes the repetitive nature of their personalities forward and lets suicide enter their psyche. The combination of thoughts of hair pulling, and ending one's life, is potentially lethal.

Urges by Gary Hennerberg

Sometimes I still blame myself. Or I realize that I can only hold myself accountable. But how do you assign accountability when there is no control?

That's what makes having an overwhelming urge like trich so frustrating. I want to stop. I want to pull. I want to blame someone or something. I pull. I pause. I'm devastated. It's a vicious circle. I want so much to be able to assign blame where blame is due. Surely I can't be held accountable for actions I can't control.

> I want to stop. I want to pull. I want to blame someone or something. I pull. I pause. I'm devastated. It's a vicious circle.

But what does that say for people who have different kinds of urges? Skin picking may only physically hurt the person who is picking their own skin. Is the person with an urge to overeat hurting themselves or others? Is the person who eats and purges physically hurting herself or is she also hurting others who love her deeply and see the self-destructive nature of this disorder? Is the man with an urge to gamble hurting himself, or is he hurting his loved ones, too, by throwing away money? And what about the person with an urge to sexually abuse children? Culturally, morally, and legally, I don't think that there is disagreement that this person must be held accountable for his or her actions and is to blame when hurting innocent children.

17 — Blame

That thought makes me pause. Pulling hair doesn't seem so bad after all.

Chapter 18
Trust God

Trust God.

I've said those two words to myself often, usually when anxiety is eating away at me. They give me comfort. Because when I examine all the troubles I've had in my life, I conclude that everything has come out all right.

The world is so much bigger than I am and has so many more issues and problems that my hair pulling urges pale in comparison.

Yet, hair pulling is a problem. It's emotionally devastating. It's physically scarring. And it molds a young person for the rest of her or his life.

Perhaps those of us with compulsive urges like trich allow this bizarre disorder to be front and center of our lives when it should be just an asterisk and a footnote. But how

> Perhaps those of us with compulsive urges like trich allow this bizarre disorder to be front and center of our lives when it should be just an asterisk and a footnote.

can you footnote a behavior that's so compulsive? How can the shame of pulling be an afterthought?

I believe there is a bigger universe than we can fathom and that God has a plan for us all.

The Bible has many passages that speak to each of us in our own way. But I have to admit that I've never been a good Bible reader. Rather, I've listened at church. I've heard the stories in sermons, or read verses in Sunday School as a child.

I don't know that I have any favorite Bible verses. But there are some that speak to me.

"I don't understand myself at all, for I really want to do what is right, but I can't. I do what I don't want to do — what I hate." The context of this verse from Romans 7:15 is about sin. So I wonder. Is hair pulling a sin?

Here's more from Romans 7:19-20.

"When I want to do good, I don't; when I try not to do wrong, I do it anyway. Now if I am doing what I don't want to, it is plain where the trouble is: sin still has me in its evil grasp."

But I prefer to be inspired by the words in Jeremiah 29: "...I will come and do for you all the good things I have promised ... for I know the plans I have for you, says the Lord. They are plans for good and not for evil, to give you a future and a hope."

There are verses that speak of hair pulling, too. I know there is context lost when reading only the Bible verse. But I find it fascinating to read of hair pulling references in the Bible.

"When I heard this, I tore my clothing and pulled hair from my head and beard and sat down utterly baffled." Ezra 9:3.

"They shave their heads and beards in anguish, and slash their hands and put on clothes of sackcloth," Jeremiah 48:37.

There are verses, too, that give me pause. These are the ones that talk of removing your hand or arm for sinning.

"The laws of Moses said, 'You shall not commit adultery.' But I say: Anyone who even looks at a woman with lust in his eye has already committed adultery with her in his heart. So if your eye — even if it is your best eye — causes you to lust, gouge it out and throw it away. Better for part of you to be destroyed than for all of you to be cast into hell. And if your hand — even your right hand — causes you to sin, cut it off and throw it away. Better that than find yourself in hell." Matthew 5:27-30.

"So if your hand or foot causes you to sin, cut it off and throw it away. Better to enter heaven crippled than to be in hell with both of your hands and feet. And if your eye causes you to sin, gouge it out and throw it away.

Urges by Gary Hennerberg

Better to enter heaven with one eye than to be in hell with two." Matthew 18:8-9.

"If your hand does wrong, cut it off. Better live forever with one hand than be thrown into the unquenchable fires of hell with two! If your foot carries you toward evil, cut it off! Better be lame and live forever than have two feet that carry you to hell." Mark 9:43-47.

Bible verses are filled with metaphors. We can interpret them to give meaning to our lives. I believe that when the words of the Bible tell me to get rid of my hand or eye that this is a figurative directive. The Bible implores us to manage our sins.

But is trich a sin? Should I literally cut off my left hand or left arm? That is the only hand I pull with. It would easily stop this mania, wouldn't it? Wouldn't it be better to destroy my hand or arm than to let trich destroy me? Would the physical pain of cutting off my hand be less than the emotional pain of pulling out my hair?

> "... I will come and do for you all the good things I have promised ... for I know the plans I have for you, says the Lord. They are plans for good and not for evil, to give you a future and a hope." — From Jeremiah 29

Or do I go back to the Jeremiah 29 when God speaks of having a plan for me?

I prefer those words of encouragement. And throughout the Bible there are words of comfort and peace. That's the God that I believe. A God of love. A God that has given me certain talents and attributes. This isn't a God of hate. God hates the sin, but still loves the sinner.

> Throughout the Bible there are words of comfort and peace. That's the God that I believe. A God of love. A God that has given me certain talents and attributes.

If trich is a sin — and I don't think that it is — then it is hated. But I know deep down that no matter what, I am loved by God.

I trust God, even in the darkest of times. I used to pray that God would help me stop pulling my hair. I used to pray that a lot. But He didn't respond. Or if He did, I didn't recognize the response. I haven't stopped pulling. No voice from heaven. No inner peace. No resolution. No guidance.

I wanted a miracle. I wanted to experience a story, like those in the Bible, of Jesus healing the sick. Jesus would heal

Urges by Gary Hennerberg

the sick because they believed. I believe! I believe in the power of God's healing power and the grace from Jesus Christ. But it doesn't feel like I've been touched or healed.

> I wonder if as a child I pulled my hair in defiance of a God that didn't answer my prayers. How could God not answer the prayer of a child?

I wonder if as a child I pulled my hair in defiance of a God that didn't answer my prayers. How could God not answer the prayer of a child?

I felt so alone.

It would have been easy for me to have stopped trusting God. But despite trich being a part of my life, I haven't abandoned my hope, my trust, or my love of God and as a Christian, the love of Jesus Christ.

> It may be our task — our life's mission — to peel back those layers of fabric one-by-one, good and bad. To accept them. To manage them. And to find inner peace to use them as part of God's plan

As an adult I now think that God gives us life on this earth to figure out how to deal with challenges. Our issues. He has a plan. He has given us strengths. And weaknesses. A weave *of fabric that envelopes us in layer after layer of complexity. It may be our task — our life's mission — to peel back those layers of fabric one-by-one, good and bad. To accept them. To manage them. And to find inner peace to use them as part of God's plan.*

CHAPTER 19
Hair Replacement

Have you ever wondered what you would look like if you could see yourself as others see you? To see the actual size of your nose and ears, the color of your eyes, and yes, the color and dimension of your hair? I find it an unpleasant thought. I doubt I'd like what I'd see.

Most of us probably do what we can to make ourselves look good. How else do we explain the flourishing sales of things like cosmetics and hair care? Or picking out clothes that fit us just right and filling our closets with more than we need? Or the proliferation of elective surgeries to take out wrinkles and waist lines?

I think we're all more vain than we want to admit. But I'll be the first to say that I think we should do what we can to enhance our appearance.

During my childhood, I did what I could to hide the bald spots. Mostly so I wouldn't be caught. But also to make myself look as good as I could. Of course, how do you explain a zany comb-over of hair? Today, whenever I see a mature man comb-over his hair from above his ear across his naturally bald head to cover it up, I ask myself, "Who does he think he's kidding? Why doesn't he just cut it normally? Or shave

Urges by Gary Hennerberg

his head? Buy a hair piece?" Just don't do the comb-over. He surely realizes that everyone knows he is bald. So why does he do it?

Having been there, I think most of us do what we can to look as natural as possible. For the baby boom generation particularly, hair has been an icon of youthfulness, power, sexual prowess and life success. And who doesn't want more of that?

> Hair has been an icon of youthfulness, power, sexual prowess and life success. And who doesn't want more of that?

My college years had been punctuated by a relatively care-free existence. I'm the first to admit I didn't study much. I worked as editor of the university newspaper. Those were the years when I learned how to write.

My first job out of college was less writing than I thought it would be. I worked as a marketing manager for a directory publishing company. My first day of work was a month from the day I had graduated, on June 19, 1978.

It was a great place to launch my career. I had a lot of latitude for someone with no marketing experience. Heck, I didn't even take a marketing course in college.

I had to move for this job. I graduated from Fort Hays State University located in Hays, Kansas. Hays is

19 — Hair Replacement

about halfway between Kansas City and Denver on the high plains of Kansas. It was a good school and a great community. It was about 200 miles from the farm where I grew up.

My first job after college was in Lincoln. I hadn't been to Lincoln much, if at all, during my college years. It was, and is, a city that always reminds me of special events in my life. Seeing the majestic state capitol. Going to stores with more choices than we had in small town stores. Yes, even the place where a doctor "outed" my hair pulling in front of my Mom and Dad. Now Lincoln would be the place where I would launch my career.

Moving to Lincoln meant significant changes. I was about a five hour drive away from my college, but most of my friends had moved away anyway. I knew no one in Lincoln. I had to rebuild a friendship base.

That first summer that I lived in Lincoln, I drove home most weekends to help Dad on the farm. This would be his first summer without me being there full-time. I knew he would need the help. Yet I also knew I had to transition from being a young adult son living at home to a young adult son living on my own. I think he knew it, too, although we never talked about it.

But for me there was another transition brewing. During the first couple of months on the job, my hair pulling got worse. Much worse.

Urges by Gary Hennerberg

I had been placed in a nice office with nice people around me, but the strain of being away from college friends, in a new town, on my first job, managing my finances, and more, made my hair pulling even worse — if that was possible.

The problem wasn't just that I was losing my hair. It was that hair was all over my desk and floor at work. That co-workers might, and probably did, see me in the act of pulling. My scalp looked horrible. There were bald spots all over, and the frenzied pulling irritated my scalp so it would be flushed red for several hours after pulling.

A couple of months after starting my new job, I realized that the only way I could deal with this was by covering it up. And by that, I mean covering it with a hair piece. A toupee.

The thought of that gave me pause. After all, how many times have we all watched a television show and seen a man wearing a toupee being made fun of with all kinds of antics. Usually the laughs were of the result of wind blowing it off, or someone innocently grabbing it and having it come off in someone else's hand. Then the audience would shriek from the yuck factor of someone holding a toupee in their hands.

> If you lived in the 1970s, you know that hair was important.

19 — Hair Replacement

I could never be that man that was made fun of in the movies and on television, but frankly, I wasn't sure I had a choice.

If you lived in the 1970s, you know that hair was important. Look at pictures of any man and you'll see a mop on his head. Look at pictures of rock stars. Watch the hit movie *Saturday Night Fever* and see John Travolta with his hair. Or the Bee Gees.

Hair wasn't just a fashion statement of the times. It was power.

And here I was destroying my "power" one strand or clump of hair at a time.

So I pulled out the phone book one day and looked for a place where I could buy a hair piece. It was difficult for me to know what to do, but I knew I had to act quickly.

> Hair wasn't just a fashion statement of the times. It was power. And here I was destroying my "power" one strand or clump of hair at a time.

It was a Friday afternoon when I was at a low point of despair when I finally picked up the phone and called one of the few places in town that advertised that they sold hair pieces. That was awkward. I don't recall what I said, but there wasn't much beating around the bush. I was calling to come in and talk to someone about hair pieces.

Urges by Gary Hennerberg

I was connected to a man named Grant. He could see me the next morning. It was the Saturday of Labor Day weekend. I agreed to the appointment time.

That morning I was excited and nervous all at the same time. I reassured myself that I didn't have to buy anything. I was only going to look. Back in those days, hair salons like this one would have an inventory of hair replacements you could try on. Today you'll probably order it custom-made.

I drove to Grant's salon across town. I was nervous. Here I was, a 21 year-old guy with a disfigured scalp looking for a rug. What would my Mom, Dad and my sisters think? My grandparents? My aunts, uncles and cousins? The people I worked with?

Oh, I thought, this really wasn't going to be easy.

I walked into the shop and told them I was there to see Grant. He was ready for me. We walked past three or four chairs into a small room. There was a curtain separating the room with the hair pieces from the rest of the shop. I knew everyone would stare. When Grant closed the curtain, I just knew it signaled to all of the customers that I was there to look at wigs.

We started with small talk to break the ice and get acquainted. Grant was very respectful and never asked me about my hair loss. Going to a barber or hair stylist was always nerve wracking for me because I was afraid

19 — Hair Replacement

of what they would ask. A few years earlier, during my freshman year of college, I went to a new hair stylist. I remember that he commented on my hair loss. It was one of the few times that I didn't lie about why it was so thin and oddly bald. I told him that I pulled it out. He freaked. Then he lectured me that I should go get some help. I never returned to that hair stylist again.

But Grant was different. Perhaps he had seen other people with hair loss like mine and knew we were pulling it out. Or perhaps he simply had the better sense to know that hair loss is traumatic and personal, and that it's better not to say anything.

He had many hair pieces lined up on shelves on his walls. About half of them were wigs for women, the other half were toupees for men. He had hair in many different colors and styles. It was almost like picking out a new shirt.

He pulled one from the shelf that was about my hair color. It was a conservative cut, with the hair parted down the left side.

Then came a moment of truth. He turned the chair away from the mirrors so I couldn't see that he was about to place it on my head. In an instant, it was there. It felt a little strange, almost like wearing a cap, except there was contact with my entire scalp. Grant combed the hair from the replacement into my own hair on the sides.

Then without fanfare or announcement, he swung the chair around to the mirror so I could see myself.

I was stunned.

For the first time I was able to look at myself in a mirror and see what I should have looked like for all these years.

It's difficult to describe what I felt at that moment. I'll always remember it. My eyes didn't well up with tears, although it wouldn't have been a surprise to me if that had happened. Rather, I just sat there looking at myself. The hair color perfectly matched my own hair. The length was just right. The style was what I likely would have worn. It was as though God had placed that hair replacement unit there for me, just waiting for the day when I would come in and try it on.

I continued to stare at myself. I thought to myself, "This is what I look like with hair. This is how I'm supposed to look." It made me look my age instead of several years older.

I liked it. It was a new me. Wearing it would be a new chapter of my life. I sat in that chair for several minutes admiring myself. Grant stood by silently, as though he knew I had to gather my thoughts. I knew in an instant I was going to buy it, but I had also promised myself that I would wait a few days before committing the money.

19 — Hair Replacement

If I bought it and started wearing it, there would be no going back.

I told Grant that I wanted to give this a few days before I would make a decision, and I asked him if he could hold this one for a week so no one else could buy it. He agreed.

That afternoon I drove down to the farm. It was Labor Day weekend so I had that following Monday off work. It would give me a chance to talk to Mom and Dad about it.

I had another concern of sorts, too. The Sunday following Labor Day was going to be my Mom and Dad's celebration of their 25th wedding anniversary. They had rented a pavilion in a park in Beatrice, about halfway between the farm and Lincoln. It would be a potluck dinner, with relatives from both sides of the family there.

It meant that in one day nearly everyone in my extended family would see me with a hair replacement. My grandparents, aunts, uncles, cousins and family friends.

I don't recall the exact conversation with Mom and Dad about my pending decision.

But Mom gave an instant approval of my decision. She thought it would be a good thing for me to do. Dad didn't say much, but by that point I figured this was more

Urges by Gary Hennerberg

a conversation telling them of my plans so they wouldn't be shocked when they saw me the next weekend.

On Tuesday, when I was back in Lincoln, I called Grant to set an appointment for the following Saturday morning. Saturday afternoon I'd head down to the farm. The next day would be the day my relatives and neighbors from the farm would see me wearing the hair replacement at my parent's 25th wedding anniversary celebration. Monday would be the first day at work everyone would see me.

I was anxious that entire week for the appointment time to arrive. I wasn't going to back out. I would have gone in earlier, but it would have meant taking time off work, and besides, I didn't want to come to work for a few hours, be out a few hours, then return with this new mop of hair on my head. There would be enough kidding or snickering behind my back, I was sure.

Saturday finally arrived and I headed back to the hair salon. Grant greeted me again and led me back to his private room and drew the curtains closed.

There it was. My new hair replacement. The new me.

I sat in the chair and he draped a cloth around me. I really didn't know what was next, other than my own hair needed to be trimmed professionally. For years I had

19 — Hair Replacement

a hair trimming device I would use to cut my hair without going to a barber since I only needed to trim the sides.

"We'll need to shave the hair off the top of your head," Grant told me. "It will make your unit fit better."

I didn't realize we'd have to do that. There wasn't much there. But it didn't matter by this point. I wasn't going to stop wearing the hair replacement so if the hair on top needed to go, then it would be shaved off.

I watched Grant shave my hair in the mirror. It was a strange sensation, feeling the shaver trim off my thinned hair with ease. It was almost as though the hair on top of my head was inconsequential. In a few seconds, it was gone. I didn't like it. And when he was finished, seeing me completely bald on top was a horrible sight.

He had put secure tape on the hair replacement so it would bond to my scalp. I was amazed at how tight the tape fit. But having watched too many TV shows and movies when the toupee blows off in the wind, my first concern was chasing my new hair down the street someday.

I had already seen how I looked the week prior, so there wasn't anything new to observe, but this time it was taped to my head and Grant had trimmed the sides of the hair piece so it would blend in perfectly with my own hair.

I felt handsome for the first time.

Urges by Gary Hennerberg

It made me feel whole. Yes, the hair was a bit too "perfect," but I didn't care. I had hair!

Grant's parting words to me I would always remember.

"This hair piece is like a cosmetic. You're wearing it to enhance your appearance. Just as people use make-up or dress well, this is a way to make you look better and feel better about yourself."

His words that may have been most important for me to hear were these: "You're not trying to fool anyone."

People would know I was wearing a hair replacement. I should acknowledge it. To pretend something hadn't changed would be phony.

Buying the hair replacement meant getting used to a few new protocols. How to secure it everyday was the most important. It required the use of special double sided tape. It was very secure. It came in rolls and I would need to cut it into strips. Remarkably, I still had the pair of scissors that Mom had given me on my first day of

19 — Hair Replacement

school. By now they were more than 15 years old, but they worked just fine.

I drove back to my apartment to pack a few things for the overnight stay on the farm, and that afternoon I made the 75 minute drive. I arrived at the farm mid-afternoon.

Mom saw me first. She said she really liked it. Still nervous, I sat down in a chair in the living room waiting for my sisters to come out from their bedroom. In an instant they turned the corner and saw me.

They just stared in silence for a few moments. They didn't know I was going to be coming home wearing a hair piece. After they got over being surprised, they seemed to be positive about it. They thought I looked younger.

Dad was outside, but it wasn't long before he saw me. He didn't say much, but I could tell he thought it was all right.

Not much was said about it. What really was there to say?

The next morning we skipped church since we were getting ready for the noon potluck. Unfortunately, the weather turned nasty and it started to rain. The potluck would be under a large pavilion in the park, but it was chilly and everyone would get wet walking from their car to the pavilion.

Urges by Gary Hennerberg

It wasn't going to be a good hair day. I drove behind my family for the 30 miles to Beatrice in my own car since I would return to Lincoln afterward on my own.

We arrived about an hour early to set up tables, put on tablecloths and get ready for the crowd. I covered my head as best as I could while dashing between the cars and pavilion to keep my hair dry.

A few minutes before noon, relatives and neighbors started to arrive.

No one seemed to notice that I had hair. That didn't disappoint me. In fact, it was a relief. But at the same time, I wondered how they could not have known. Yet these were people I didn't see very often so they may have thought I had simply let my hair grow out now that I was living on my own.

My Grandma Cacek, Mom's mother, knew right away and she complimented me on it. But not much was said. That was good.

My cousin Jerry, who was only six months younger than me, and a year behind me in school, was home from college that weekend. We didn't talk at first, but suddenly he came up to me.

"I didn't recognize you, Gary," he said. "I kept looking and wondering who that was over there and I finally figured it was you!" He didn't point out that it was

19 — Hair Replacement

because of the hair. He didn't have to. I took all of it as a compliment.

By the end of the afternoon, I felt better about my decision. A few people made positive comments, even if only to say that I looked nice. But most didn't say a word. It was me who was worried about what they would think, but most people didn't notice. That's the way I wanted it.

Monday morning at work I figured would be different. How could people who saw me on Friday, going bald, not notice that on Monday I had thick brown perfectly combed hair.

But no one snickered, at least to my face. There were comments such as "you look good," "it's a new Gary," and other positive things. Thankfully again, it seemed to be mostly a non-event. I have no question there were people saying things behind my back. But I figured those comments could be no worse than talking about my weird bald pattern and red scalp. Or how they may have caught a glimpse of me pulling hair.

And who knows. Maybe they all knew I was a hair puller and my secret wasn't a secret at all.

But from those days forward, until one day in 2007, I would wear a hair replacement and not dare be seen without one. That would have been the worst humiliation of all.

Urges by Gary Hennerberg

From that September weekend in 1978, I would wear a hair replacement for over 28 years. It was my cover.

I didn't know what to expect as far as my urges to pull would be concerned. But something pleasant happened. When I wore my hair piece, I had absolutely no urge to pull hair. I wouldn't sneak a hair from the side. I didn't ever pull my eye lashes or eye brows. But I did pull other hair on my body. I was ashamed of how my chest appeared so I didn't take off my shirt. Going swimming would now be difficult with both wearing a hair piece and having a disfigured chest of hair.

But the urges to pull hair from my head had been eliminated.

That always puzzled me. Why would covering up my hair stop me? But the moment I removed my hair piece before bedtime, the frenzy could start. And when I would awaken in the morning, I'd almost always reach up and pull out a few hairs. Perhaps it was a way for me to wake up. Or more likely, it was a manifestation of a lifetime of pulling. It was just me. Part of the complex fabric of my soul and being.

19 — Hair Replacement

But mostly it didn't matter to me. I was wearing a hair replacement and I looked almost natural.

And there is one other part of this story worth mentioning. The scissors — the ones given to me by my Mom on my first day of school — would be used for all the years I wore a hair replacement to cut tape. Those scissors gave me comfort.

But I almost had to give them up one day. It was September, 2001, the first day airplanes were allowed to fly after the 9/11 terrorist attacks. The rules at airport security had changed. This particular trip was to be just overnight to meet a prospective client. As I passed through security, they pulled out my overnight pack and said I couldn't take the scissors onboard. The scissors had curved ends and couldn't possibly pose the threat of a weapon, but it was pointless to argue.

There were no options. I couldn't take it with me and airport security would dispose of it. No one could possibly have understood what that pair of scissors meant to me. I

Urges by Gary Hennerberg

asked the security people if I could turn around and check it. They let me make an about face back to the check-in counter.

Everyone that day at the airport was still shocked with the events of 9/11, so when I asked the man at the counter if I could check my scissors, he probably thought it was peculiar. My overnight carry-on wasn't conducive to checking or I would have done that. But the American Airlines ticket agent found a small box, about the size of a lunch bucket, that the scissors could be placed in. He taped the box shut and it was placed on the conveyor belt and I prayed that my beloved scissors would make it.

Thankfully, this story has a happy ending. My scissors made it. There was hardly anyone on the flight that day so there was little luggage checked. My scissors were spinning on the carousel to be picked up when we arrived. Knowing I would experience the same issue for my return trip, I asked for an envelope at the front desk of my hotel, bought stamps, and then carefully taped those scissors to a piece of paper and put them in the envelope to be mailed to me. And yes, a couple of days later my cherished scissors had arrived home.

CHAPTER 20
Love of Life

Everyone needs someone special in their lives. As children, it's our parents. As adults, it's a spouse, lover, partner or best friend. It's an added bonus when you can use the words spouse, lover, partner and best friend to describe the same person.

As we enter our late teen years and early adult years the transition begins from the center of the universe being your parents to someone new out there in the world. I can't speak for everyone who has trich, but I wonder if our transition may be more difficult than it is for others. If the bond with our parents is so strong — and mine was and is today — that it's tough to find someone with whom you can be intimate.

I can't imagine anyone with trich wanting to be "outed" because of a relationship gone badly. It's a secret. A very deep secret. It's extremely difficult to acknowledge it to anyone. Especially someone you've fallen in love with because you fear chasing that special someone away with the revelation that you're a hair puller. It's a risk for anyone with trich to engage in a relationship.

I've discovered through conversations with other hair pullers that a deep paranoia exists of how to hide trich from

Urges by Gary Hennerberg

your mate. I've met women at trichotillomania conferences who have told their husbands that they were out-of-town with friends, hiding the fact they had gone to a trich event. I've met single people who are afraid of starting a relationship for fear of being discovered and devastated if that special someone dumps them because of trich.

> Trich is that invisible elephant in the room for us hair pullers. We don't want to talk about it but we see it even if others in the same room don't.

Trich is that invisible elephant in the room for us hair pullers. We don't want to talk about it but we see it even if others in the same room don't.

So how do you deal with a budding relationship? I, for one, didn't date in high school. I was too shy, too afraid of being discovered, too tall, you name it. I had every excuse in the book. I went to my high school prom by myself. And the night of high school graduation, when my class had a party, I didn't go. I was a loner. And in many respects I still am.

By the time I got to college, I started dating. Perhaps I had grown up just a little more and had a little more confidence in myself. But there was always that nagging issue of whether or not to ever speak of my hair pulling with newly made friends. I didn't. It was too weird. Too awkward to ever bring up. How do you steer the conversation such that you add, "oh, by the way, I really like you but I wanted to tell you that I pull my hair?"

I think if you observe the mood of the moment there will come an unexpected time when it's a natural discussion. You then reveal your deepest secret and pray for acceptance. Or you say nothing and pursue the lonely fork in the road that you've chosen to take.

―✑―

In college I met my wife, LoCinda. She doesn't remember meeting me. So much for first impressions! She was the student secretary to the chairman of the Speech Department at Fort Hays State University. We were friends throughout college, often bumping into each other on campus. Eventually we lived down the hall from one another in the same coed residence hall.

After college, LoCinda went her own way to work in Iowa. With me in Lincoln, we were a couple hundred miles apart but stayed in touch. We visited each other often. For a couple of those years, Frontier Airlines had a flight that stopped in Lincoln and then Des Moines as part of a flight out of Denver. It was cheap to fly it. We've often joked that we could credit Frontier Airlines for keeping us together.

Three years after college, it was apparent we were more than just friends. I think it was that friendship that

Urges by Gary Hennerberg

has given us a rock-solid marriage. LoCinda really is my best friend, my buddy, my pal. We were married in 1982.

She knew me before the hair replacement. At the time I got the hair replacement, we had only graduated from FHSU about four months earlier. We were at that stage in our relationship when we had emerged from being just friends to something closer.

I vividly recall the occasion when she first saw me with my hair replacement. I don't know what word to use to describe this time in our lives. We were friends, but I think we both sensed there was something more to our relationship than just that. We kept in touch, but we didn't see each other very often. When we talked by phone, I didn't say anything about getting the hair replacement, and I certainly never revealed that I pulled my hair.

One cold and snowy night later that winter, LoCinda was driving from her parents' home in Kansas back to Iowa. Her drive took her through Lincoln and she stopped by to visit. It was then that I greeted her at the door of my apartment with a full head of dark hair. I think she was so struck, or perhaps tired and stressed from the drive, that she made only a passing comment. I did what I could to rescue the moment and make an awkward joke about my new hair.

It would be later in the evening that I finally told her my long deeply held secret. I remember little of the conversation, but what I do recall is how I was surprised with how it didn't matter to her. Or maybe it was so freaky that she preferred to ignore it and thought I was delusional!

At that time, LoCinda was one of only a handful of people whom I had ever told of my hair pulling urges. I wanted her to know early on in case it would scare her away from me. Thankfully, **it didn't.**

LoCinda doesn't remember much of the conversation either. And when I asked her to pen her thoughts about it for this book, she said this:

"If there's anything I want Gary to realize after twenty six years of marriage, it's that I see him as so much more than just someone who pulls his hair. The world does not define him as a hair puller, and neither

"If there's anything I want Gary to realize after twenty six years of marriage, it's that I see him as so much more than just someone who pulls his hair. The world does not define him as a hair puller, and neither do I. He was first my friend, then my husband, then the father of my children. He still is the light of my life."

Urges by Gary Hennerberg

do I. He was first my friend, then my husband, then the father of my children. He still is the light of my life."

In the months that followed, we became closer and closer. I introduced her to my family. She introduced me to her family.

In 1981, I decided it was time to advance my career. Because the career prospects in my area of specialization were few in Lincoln, I realized it could mean moving elsewhere. Besides, I was young enough to have wanderlust in my heart and wanted to move around to see and experience more of the country. That put LoCinda and I at a crossroads. I interviewed for a job in Des Moines, where she lived, but it didn't pan out. So I expanded my search. And even though we weren't yet engaged, I asked if she wanted to remain in Des Moines, or make a move to the city where I would end up. To my delight, and relief, she opted to move wherever I would go.

In June of 1981 we moved to Cheyenne, Wyoming. On October 31, I asked LoCinda to marry me. I was scared she would say "no." She quickly said "yes" and asked what took me so long!

We were married on May 8, 1982, in Washington, Kansas, just a few blocks away from the high school where so many of my 4-H activities had taken place. Even though we were living in Cheyenne and had made some friends there (and later moved to other places in the country, before settling in Texas in 1991), we wanted to be married close to family.

Our wedding day is one I'll always treasure and cherish. The springtime weather was perfect. We were surrounded by our family. It was its own fairy tale wedding for us two twentysomethings from rural and humble roots. And we have been blessed to have had two beautiful daughters, Amy and Liza.

I count my blessings that somewhere along the way I found love. I have been blessed that LoCinda has accepted me and my personality. A personality which I believe has been profoundly shaped by my obsession with hair pulling. Where everything must be in its place in certain areas of my life, but total chaos in other places. That I must check and recheck things like door locks. Sweeping and vacuuming hair from the most unlikely of places. How when I removed my hair replacement before going to bed my disfigured bald head was exposed. That was a sight repugnant to me, and if it ever was to LoCinda, she never uttered a word.

She watched helplessly as I would pull my hair within minutes of awakening. And at night she heard me tear out hair before falling asleep. If I was especially stressed, the pulling would last for several minutes, the evidence would be found on the pillow and floor next to me.

How did I rate to find my angel on earth? Someone who would accept me and love me weirdly bald and all?

I go back to my faith, a faith I don't always understand. I believe it was meant to be. While in high school I felt a strong pull to go to FHSU. But for my first year of college I went to a different school in Missouri, even dating a wonderful young woman there. My heart continued to pull me to FHSU where I transferred for my sophomore year. LoCinda and I met almost the first day I was there. While she may not remember that meeting, I certainly do. It wasn't love at first sight. It was bonding at first sight. That magical moment when that sixth sense opens up and you know this is a person you want to have in your life.

> It wasn't love at first sight. It was bonding at first sight. That magical moment when that sixth sense opens up and you know this is a person you want to have in your life.

CHAPTER 21
Generations

While growing up, I never thought about hair pulling as something that could have been genetic. After all, I believed I was the only person on the planet who pulled hair.

But research suggests there could be a link between generations and that trich is genetic. I don't know. I've heard of mothers who pull hair who have daughters who pull hair. It happens.

So I've wondered from time-to-time if it was possible there was a genetic link in my family. I don't think there was. My parents aren't hair pullers. And while I really don't think my grandparents were either, the fact remains, though, that those of us who pull hair are experts at hiding it from virtually everyone.

> Research suggests there could be a link between generations and that trich is genetic.

I was blessed to have all four of my grandparents as a part of my childhood. We were all close to each other, and I'd say that I saw them at some point nearly every week of my growing up years. It was remarkable to me that I had all four of my grandparents as part of my life until I was 25, when my first grandparent died. My last surviving grandparent died when I was 37.

My paternal grandparents lived only about 2.5 miles from us, even though they lived in Nebraska and we lived in Kansas. They were farmers, too. My Dad, Alvin, was their oldest of five boys, Lyle, Ervin, Larry and Dennis. One brother died at birth. Dad, Lyle, Ervin and Dennis were farmers. Larry went on to be a high school teacher.

My paternal grandmother was as dear to me as any grandmother could be. She was a farmer's wife. She loved to cook and garden. Or maybe because of the era of her life there was no real choice as a farmer's wife except to keep a garden and cook.

Her homemade bread was delicious. She used special yeast that gave the bread a flavor that would melt in your mouth. No one, no where, has ever made homemade bread exactly like my Grandma Hennerberg.

Her garden was big and perfectly kept every summer. My favorite thing? Strawberries fresh from her garden. She also made rhubarb pie with rhubarb from her garden. No one could make a rhubarb pie like my Grandma.

Grandpa was a farmer of German descent. In my early years as a child, we baled hay together. Grandpa wasn't known as a patient man. He always drove the car. Grandma never learned how to drive. Regularly when

21 — Generations

they would go somewhere she would get in the car and before she could close the door he would put the car in gear and drive away. It's a wonder she never fell out all those years.

He had chickens. I remember helping him gather eggs sometimes. But he wasn't one to say a lot. I saw my grandparents in church every Sunday. We worked together on the farm. We shared many meals together. We spent every Christmas Eve together at their house for years and years. A cherished gift is a quilt my Grandmother made. One Christmas she gave all of us grandkids — my cousins and me — a quilt. There were at least a dozen of us (some may have been born after this particular Christmas). She had us draw numbers from a basket, and then she went to her extra bedroom and gave us the quilt with the corresponding number. I don't recall my age, but I must have been in college, maybe even out of college, by then. My grandmother had spent that entire year making quilts for us grandkids. What a gift! What a legacy!

> My grandmother had spent that entire year making quilts for us grandkids. What a gift! What a legacy! To this day I sleep with that quilt — symbolic of the complex weave of fabric of my mind — on my bed.

Urges by Gary Hennerberg

To this day I sleep with that quilt — symbolic of the complex weave of fabric of my mind — on my bed. It will surely last my entire lifetime and I'll use it until the threads are bare. But thankfully, even after at least 30 years of use, the quilt endures today. And I think of my Grandmother nearly every morning while making our bed. Grandpa Hennerberg died in 1983, and Grandma died in 1994.

My maternal grandparents, Grandpa and Grandma Cacek — a Czech name pronounced "saw sick" — lived about 15 miles away. That seemed like a long distance, but of course, it really wasn't. They, too, were farmers. My Mom, Elaine, had a sister, Charlene, and two brothers, Arnold and Virgil. Arnold lived at home with my grandparents. He was a life-long bachelor, had served in World War II in Japan, and had photos — all in slides so he could show them with a projector — that he had taken while there. They fascinated me, and I wish he were alive to show them to me again. Arnold died in his 50s from pancreatic cancer. My uncle Virgil and his family moved to Maryville, Missouri, when I was a teen. I went to college for a year in Maryville at Northwest Missouri State University and worked weekends at my uncle's drive-in restaurant, the Arctic Circle. Virgil died young as well, of lung cancer. At one time I was close to his five kids — my cousins — when we would have Sunday noon-time dinner together at our grandparents. That was before they moved to Missouri.

My grandparents would often host all of us, my uncles, aunts and cousins, at their home for dinner. In fact, for a few years it seemed we went to their home nearly every Sunday, if not for dinner, then at least for the afternoon.

My Grandpa Cacek was a tall man, perhaps 6'5", as was most of my family. I grew to be the tallest at 6'8".

My Grandpa and Grandma loved to go fishing. For a couple of summers, when I was somewhere between about seven and ten years old, they would take me along with my two older cousins, Lynn and Dean, on a weeklong fishing trip to Minnesota. We'd stay in small, rustic cabins on lakes. The fishing was usually good, but it was the time together that was so special to me.

Years later, when they were retired, they would drive to my Dad's farms where we had four ponds in the pastures, and the Little Blue River that came through one of the farms on the Kansas side of the state line. This is the point where the Little Blue left Nebraska and entered Kansas. We didn't always catch many fish, but some days were more notable than others. Grandpa died in 1981.

I was close to my Grandma Cacek. I think she knew before anyone else that I pulled my hair. She never said a word, at least that I can remember, about it. She always

Urges by Gary Hennerberg

made me, and I think my sisters and cousins, too, feel very special. She had a gift of drawing you to her.

In 1973 she suffered a major heart attack. She survived, but it took her years to get better and she never fully recovered. Despite that major set-back, she lived until 1988, dying only five months before our first daughter was born. How I wanted my Grandmother to be able to hold our daughter, Amy. She lived by herself and apparently had another heart attack one morning, for she was found in her night clothes. Regrettably, she wasn't found for a couple of days. When it came time for the funeral, there wouldn't be an open casket to be able to see her and say a final good-bye.

> She didn't like her hair. I didn't like my hair either ... I'll never know why or if there was something she was trying to tell me.

She seemed to always have extra compassion for me. I know that she was sensitive to the fact that I pulled my hair. I recall one day the two of us talked about wavy brown hair and how difficult it was to care for it. She didn't like her hair. I didn't like my hair either ... I'll never know why she didn't like her hair or if there was something she was trying to tell me.

21 — Generations

Over the years I've observed our daughters touching and twirling their hair as teenagers sometimes do. I think it's fairly natural for people to touch their hair. Any time over the years when I've seen them touching their hair, usually while reading a book or watching television, my heart races.

Until Amy and Liza were 18 and 14, I hadn't told them that I pulled my hair. I was afraid to. I was afraid that the suggestion would somehow encourage them or give them permission to start pulling, too. I knew the devastation that hair pulling had caused in my life and I couldn't bear to see that happen to them, too. There is research to suggest that trichotillomania can be genetically passed from generation to generation. That it could be genetic continues to concern me. Whether it's my daughters, or if they have children of their own, I'm worried about it continuing on. Passing this wretched disorder on to future generations worries me. I've lived with it, but not everyone copes and is able to go on with normal lives. I pray trichotillomania stops with me.

> Passing this wretched disorder on to future generations worries me. I've lived with it, but not everyone copes and is able to go on with normal lives. I pray trichotillomania stops with me.

Chapter 22
Reinventing Myself

There came a point when I decided that I needed to gut it up and deal with trichotillomania. It wasn't an "ah ha!" moment. It came over time. I long ago accepted that the urge to pull my hair was forever woven into my fabric. I had felt shame. I had prayed. There seemingly wasn't an answer to my prayers, but to think so would sell God short. I had been asking God to make me stop pulling. I hadn't asked God for guidance to accept myself as He had woven me. I hadn't asked God to help me overcome shame. I hadn't been thankful for my gifts and talents. I had dwelled on my hair pulling urges when I should have looked at the good things in my life.

Urges by Gary Hennerberg

Over the years I have come to accept myself. I had struggled with pushing back at my urges when it wouldn't change things. I resisted when I should have embraced.

Slowly I decided that it was time to lift the veil, and just be who I am: A guy who happens to pull his hair.

―⁂―

I had wanted to write my childhood story as a hair puller for quite some time. There was a time that I said I would first write the book, and then take the daring step of peeling off my hairpiece, shaving my head and going on with life.

Those events have all happened, but not in that sequence.

Over the years I had thought every once in a while about shaving my head and moving on. I never seriously considered it because it was too frightening. What would people think? Would I lose face with business associates? Would people around me think that I'm a weirdo? A freak?

Shaving my head would reveal the physical scars of decades of hair pulling. Everyone would be able to see the strange lines and patterns where there is hair and smooth skin. My scalp would be a patch-work quilt. Not very handsome. But it would be me.

LoCinda had known for years that I was a hair puller. Our daughters never knew. I didn't want them to know at too young of an age fearing they may get the idea themselves that somehow they had permission to pull their hair. Only a handful of close friends were ever told.

There were a series of events that finally prodded me to shave my head. In 2005, when I turned age 49, I realized that in a year I would hit one of those major milestones in life, the big "five-o." I looked at myself in the mirror and realized that there were many things I had done to hold myself back physically because of hair pulling. I hadn't been a swimmer. While I had gone to the gym over the years, I would always sport a ball cap instead of my hairpiece. It was too hot to wear it. I was never in great physical shape.

At my annual physical before my 49th birthday I weighed more than I had ever weighed in my life. I had ballooned up to 259 pounds. While I'm 6'8" tall, most people may not have noticed my extra pounds. But I knew I was overweight. I had walked for exercise for years, but it was apparent that wasn't enough.

I decided to find a personal trainer for weight lifting. I had always been concerned about finding the right person with the right skills, someone who wouldn't push a person like me too hard and injure me. I searched, and I found a guy who demonstrated to me that we could work together. His name was Rod. He was self-exemplifying in that he was in outstanding shape, in his late 50s, but he

Urges by Gary Hennerberg

looked more like he was in his early 40s. He could see that I needed to shed a few pounds. I signed up for workouts three times a week in his studio.

I wore a ball cap to my sessions with him. But laying down on benches, sweating, and moving around as I did, it became apparent after a few weeks that wearing the cap was ridiculous. So one day, when I felt the moment was right, I pulled off my cap to reveal my chopped up and disfigured scalp. I didn't have to tell him I was bald. He had figured that out long before. I told Rod that I pulled my hair. Didn't matter to him. He was an ex-military guy who had seen and met a lot of people over the years. He also had a no-nonsense point of view with people.

> "Just shave it off," he snapped. "No one cares about what you look like. It's what's inside. Besides, lots of guys shave their heads, some aren't even bald, and they look great."

"Just shave it off," he snapped. "No one cares about what you look like. It's what's inside. Besides, lots of guys shave their heads, some aren't even bald, and they look great."

After several weeks of working out I had shed around 10 pounds. I could see that he was training me to get exactly the results that I had wanted. I kept working and working and by the summer of 2006 had lost over 25 pounds.

In a few months, I had reinvented my physique. Not completely, mind you. I hardly became a muscle stud. But at least I lost the fat and started to see some semblance of definition.

Rod encouraged me to shave my head from time-to-time. He didn't mention it often. But once in a while when he sensed the time was appropriate, he'd give me a nudge.

The push that put me over the edge to shave my head came from an unlikely place. In the fall of 2006, my wife and daughters were captivated by the television show *Dancing with the Stars*. I found myself drawn into it as well. The final three contestants featured three men: Mario Lopez, Joey Lawrence, and Emmett Smith. They were described on the show as "two bald guys and a set of dimples."

In the final days of the show, viewers and people in the audience where interviewed. There were several women who swooned over the bald guys, saying how sexy they looked. Now, I didn't have delusions that women would swoon over me if I were to shave my head. But it was an important validation for me to hear that women, and I suppose men, too, like the look of a completely bald, or shaved, head.

Urges by Gary Hennerberg

    I thought about shaving my head every day in those final days of *Dancing with the Stars*. A few weeks earlier I had celebrated my 50th birthday and there was something going on in my mind that was pushing me to do it. Emmett Smith, a bald man who happens to be a great dancer and football player, won the contest. I came to a conclusion: I, too, would shave my head. I wouldn't do it immediately, but I would think it through, imagine myself completely shaved, have time to tell a few people what I was doing, and have a specific date when I would do it.

    One evening I pulled LoCinda aside and told her that I had decided to shave my head. She was shocked. She had heard me mention that I was thinking of doing it every once in a while over the years. But this time was different. I had made the decision.

    I decided I wanted to wait until after the Thanksgiving and Christmas season had passed. There would be too much pressure and stress to do it at that time of year.

    I decided to shave my head on February 1st. That was a Thursday. Thursday nights were chorus rehearsals for me. I would shave my head after returning from rehearsal on Thursday night and then make sure to plan no meetings or interaction with people I knew on Friday. I wanted time to get used to this new look.

By the time my decision had been made it was early November. It would give me about three months to anticipate the day I would shave my head. Time to tell my family and a few close friends. Time to get used to what was going to be a new chapter in my life.

I said nothing about my plans to anyone during November and December. But I started to make a short list of people whom I would tell.

In the meantime, I decided to let my moustache and a goatee grow out. It would give me a new look that I had never done before. I didn't want my head and face to be totally hairless. I started to let it grow in December. It looked good, but it was tough not pulling the hair on my chin. Several people commented on the moustache and goatee, not knowing that in a few weeks my hair would be gone.

I wanted to tell our daughters, Amy and Liza, before I would tell anyone else. They needed to know. There would be no scheduling or rehearsing this speech. I just had to sense when the time would be right and ease into the conversation. That's exactly what happened one evening after a family dinner sometime in January. I don't recall what we were talking about or how I steered us there. But LoCinda knew in an instant what I was doing.

The girls were surprised. But they didn't seem shocked. I explained to them that hair pulling had been part of my life since the age of 6 and there was nothing in my power to stop it. They asked a few questions, but for the most part it was drama-free and a non-event.

LoCinda and I met our friends Debbie and Jay over dinner a couple of weeks before I shaved my head. Telling them was nerve-wracking. But I knew they would understand. It was an opportunity to answer their questions, knowing their questions would be similar to that of so many people. At the end of dinner, our friendship remained. I told my friend, Jeff, of my plans and my trainer, Rod.

I told Rick, one of the pastors at our church. Another day I met another long-time friend, Tom. Both of them took the news in stride. They listened. They didn't judge me. They accepted me for who I am.

As I told a handful of people it became more and more apparent that this part of me — this crazy urge to pull my hair — didn't make a difference in our friendship. I think they saw it for what it is: a medical mystery. And that this mystery had profoundly molded me into who I am.

I needed to tell Mom and Dad. With them in Nebraska and my family in Texas, I waited to tell them until after I had shaved my head since they wouldn't see me right away after doing it.

22 — Reinventing Myself

As the February 1 "shave date" neared, I became more and more comfortable with my decision. I bought a pair of hair clippers. I needed them to trim my moustache and goatee and they would be just right for shaving off my hair. I was prepared.

Chorus rehearsal that night was typical. This would be the last time the guys I sing with would see me with hair, but I wasn't going to tell them. My "re-entry" at the first chorus meeting a couple of weeks later as a completely bald man was going to be tough. I'll tell you about that experience in the next chapter.

While at rehearsal, it was with eager anticipation over the evening as in silence I thought about what I would do when I arrived home. LoCinda would be waiting up for me to help out. When rehearsal wrapped up at about 10:30, I dashed away to head home.

LoCinda was waiting. She said, "You're really going to do this, aren't you?" There was no going back in my mind.

> I flicked the on button on the clippers and started shaving on my left side — the side where I had always pulled the most. There was a symbolism, perhaps, to shave there first. Maybe it was revenge. ⁓

Urges by Gary Hennerberg

We went into our bathroom where there are large mirrors. I pulled out a chair so I could sit and we could shave my head. But first, I wanted to shave the sides.

I peeled off my hairpiece and looked at myself in the mirror one last time before I would dramatically change my appearance. I flicked the on button on the clippers and started shaving on my left side — the side where I had always pulled the most. There was a symbolism, perhaps, to shave there first. Maybe it was revenge. Certainly, this was an emotional experience.

I was surprised at how easily the hair cascaded off my head and onto my shoulder. I kept going. It felt good. I knew I wouldn't be able to pull my scalp hair again.

In about two minutes, we had shaved it all off. I used my razor to shave it down closer.

Then I just stared at myself. Like the day in 1978 when I had put on my hair replacement for the first time, I now saw myself *au natural*. No hair of my own. No hairpiece. Just me. Bald me.

I took a deep breath. I wasn't sure that I liked what I saw at first. But there was no going back.

The next day I went shopping for a hat. No one at the mall paid any attention to me. The sales person at the store didn't treat me any differently than any other customer. I found a black hat. A Stetson. It looked really good. I had never worn a hat before, so this, too, would be part of my new life. The hat made me look distinguished. It gave me new character. It was a new layer I could put on my head from time to time.

That evening we went out for dinner. I wore my new hat. No one cared or noticed.

Sunday at church all three pastors said very encouraging words to me. Rick had my permission to mention my decision to other pastoral staff. He knew that this was going to be a challenging time for me, and I could sense that they had said prayers on my behalf that week. Friends from church stopped and told me they liked the new look. One lady pulled LoCinda aside and said I looked "hot." Made my head swell. Another lady asked me why I shaved off all that beautiful hair. She never knew it was fake.

But after all of this, I still hadn't told my Mom and Dad or sisters. Dad and Mom had retired in 1994. They bought a home in Fairbury, a few blocks from the hospital where I was born. They've lived there ever since and have enjoyed a long and fulfilling retirement. I'm so happy for them.

I wouldn't be seeing them until late-February during a business trip back to Nebraska so I decided it would be easiest to write a letter to them explaining what I had done. A phone call just didn't seem like it would work for me. Awkward silences. Questions. So I wrote a letter,

Urges by Gary Hennerberg

which happened to coincide with when I would send a birthday card to my Mom. This is what I wrote:

It's been an interesting and exciting past couple of weeks for me. After a lot of thought, I decided it was time to stop wearing my hair replacement and instead just shave my head. Yup, it's now completely shaved. Lots of guys do it these days and it looks good. I shaved it on Feb. 1. So, when I see you on Sunday the 25th, I'm going to look a lot different than you're used to. I've let the moustache and goatee grow out, and I've had many people tell me it's a very good look for me. It's taking some getting used to, of course, but each day gets better and better.

By the time the day came for me to arrive in Fairbury, I felt good about myself. It had been over three weeks since I had shaved my head. I flew into Omaha and drove the two and a half hours to Fairbury. It was a cold February morning. I was glad I had worn my hat.

Pulling up in the driveway I had an eager anticipation. I think Mom and Dad did, too. I left my hat on as I walked to the front door. They were there to greet me. We hugged, but they didn't say a word about my hair.

"Are you ready to see the new me?" I asked. They were ready. Like a magician pulling a rabbit out of a hat, I swiftly removed my hat from my head. They stared for a moment. They liked it. Dad thought it made me look younger. Mom warmed up to it. I knew it would take some getting used to. They had known me from the moment I was born and had watched me grow up and slowly change. But this was a dramatic change with little warning or notice. My sisters and their families eventually saw me, too, and for the most part, after the initial shock of it everyone has moved on. Which is exactly what I had hoped would happen.

Shaving my head has enriched my life. For months I would meet someone I hadn't seen for some time and surprise them with my new look. The positive comments flowed. While I have no doubt there were those who didn't care for the look and didn't say anything one way or another, there were so many genuinely positive things said that I haven't regretted this decision. In fact, I wish I had done it years sooner.

> Shaving my head has enriched my life.

CHAPTER 23

Turning Point

The weeks leading up to my decision to shave my head were filled with anxious anticipation. One day I was excited and wanted to do it immediately. Other moments I was scared about how my family, friends, associates and people around me would react.

And what would the guys I sing with every week think?

In 1993, I joined a singing organization based in Dallas named The Vocal Majority Chorus. As part of the Barbershop Harmony Society, it's an all-male chorus singing barbershop-style and other types of music. The VM, as it's called, has won multiple Gold Medals in International Chorus Competition, several of which I'm proud to have earned as part of the chorus. The VM has excelled at performing four-part harmony with other musical styles, too, and is called America's Premier Pops Chorus. The 120 or so members are like brothers to me.

We rehearse every Thursday evening. The first Thursday rehearsal I could attend after shaving my head would be a recording session. That day, I strong-armed

Urges by Gary Hennerberg

our Associate Director, Greg Clancy, into meeting me for lunch so I could break the news to him.

Greg's father, Jim Clancy, was one of the founding members of VM in 1972 and serves as Musical Director. Jim is a man with style and grace. A champion. A natural born leader. When you speak with him, you feel as if you're the only person in the universe who matters to him. Clearly he is a role model for combining success with a winning personality. Every year at a special banquet the Vocal Majority gives out awards to members who have contributed extra time to the betterment of the organization. One of those awards is named the Jim Clancy Award for Outstanding Contributions to the Performing Chorus. I was shocked one evening at our annual banquet when I was announced as the winner of that award for 1999. It may be the most cherished award I've ever been given because of Jim's name on the award.

Jim's son, Greg, is like his father. I wanted to show Greg my shaved look before the recording session that evening and talk to him individually about what I had done. For weeks I had struggled with whether I should get up in front of the guys and tell them, or just leave it alone and shrug off the comments. That morning, I had decided to keep my story private except to tell Greg, Jim and perhaps a handful of other guys.

23 — Turning Point

Greg was already seated at the restaurant when I arrived dressed in black turtleneck, black jeans, and my new black hat.

He looked up somewhat sheepishly and asked, "What have you done?" It was apparent the hair on the sides of my head was shaved, but the top was concealed by my hat.

I don't recall exactly what I said. My heart was racing so fast. But rather than answer his question directly, I simply removed my hat. And Greg's eyes nearly popped out.

I shared with him my story and my decision. I told him that it wasn't a secret anymore, that I pull my hair, but that I probably would keep it quiet with the guys.

It was a strange lunch. I was nervous. Greg was so stunned that I don't think he knew how to react. That was exactly my greatest fear: that my friends would be so taken aback that they wouldn't know what to say and I'd be left wondering if they thought I was crazy. And if I was about to lose all my friends. We parted that day after lunch saying we'd see each other in a few hours, but I found myself almost dazed as I left. Even in fear. It was the first time I had any misgivings about shaving my head.

That evening, the recording session would be for our next Christmas CD. It seemed strange to be recording for Christmas in February, but it was just after our

Urges by Gary Hennerberg

annual Christmas Shows and we were familiar with our new songs.

The name of the CD had already been selected, and tonight we would record the title song, *Believe*. You may recognize it from the movie, *The Polar Express*. The song's lyrics tell us we have everything we need in life if we just believe, and the words encourage us to give our dreams the wings to fly.

I found myself drawn to the lyrics, "destinations are where we begin again." On this recording night, I had arrived at a destination of sorts. It was a time where I could begin again. This was a night when perhaps 120 guys would see me for the first time with my head shaved. I had prayed that my friends — my VM brothers — would still accept me. But perhaps I would find them drifting away from me and I'd have to begin making new friends again.

> I had arrived at a destination of sorts. It was a time where I could begin again.

The church where we recorded was about a 25 minute drive from my home. It was acoustically wonderful, the reason we selected this particular location.

I had left a few minutes later than I had intended. Partly just because I was running late, but partly because I was procrastinating a bit. And I didn't really want to arrive

23 — Turning Point

early and have to jump into conversations about my new look.

As I walked in the church, the chorus was at the front of the church, in the choir loft, warming up.

I donned my black uniform for the day, including the black hat and a new black pea coat LoCinda had given me for Christmas. The chorus was busy warming up so they weren't paying attention to me and other late arrivers. At least I don't think so. But I strode in from the side, walked toward the front of the church where I took off my pea coat and hat and placed them in an empty pew toward the front of the church.

There I was now. Exposed.

If anyone happened to have looked up they would see me, but I didn't make any eye contact.

Fortunately, there was a way to the choir loft from the side of the sanctuary up a flight of stairs that kept me from being seen. I emerged at the top of the stairs and paused. My heart was racing. Then I took a breath and walked into the choir loft. I knew if I stopped that it would make this all the more traumatic.

I kept my head down as I weaved through a few guys standing in the back couple of rows to take my place toward the center.

Urges by Gary Hennerberg

I took my place and looked up at Greg, who was warming up the chorus. A handful of guys looked over at me.

I smiled. But deep down was mortified.

Through the remainder of the warm-up, some of the guys would look over at me.

But something amazing happened. Those who could see me smiled. They would wave. Some even gave me a thumbs up.

I suppose it was enough of a distraction for Greg that after a few minutes he made light of the situation, in a positive kind of way, and made a comment to the entire chorus about the "new Gary" in the back row.

About a hundred guys turned to look at me. I smiled, waved, and we went on with the warm-up. In a few minutes we divided into our voice part sections to rehearse *Believe*.

The bass section, about 40 of us, would walk to the choir room down the hall.

As we walked to the choir room, many paused and asked me about my new look. The questions were many and sincere.

"Why did you do this?"

"Are you okay?"

And several told me they liked the new look. The concern and positive reinforcement eased my concerns

23 — Turning Point

somewhat, but the questions kept coming. I wanted to start to tell them, but how do you blurt out "Well, I pull my hair out so I decided to shave off what little bit I had left?"

After our 20 minute or so sectional rehearsal we headed back to the sanctuary. The questions and comments as we walked back to the sanctuary kept coming. And I sensed there were a lot of guys who wanted to ask or say something, but they were holding back.

I decided I couldn't keep this private. So before we started to record, I went up to Greg and told him that at some point in the evening, when he thought it would be best, that I'd like a few minutes to stand before the guys and share with them my story. He agreed.

We started recording *Believe*, and while there was the usual stop and go, the music and singing were glorious.

I sensed my face and smile more expressive than with any song I had ever sung. The words brought out a radiance in me I had never felt before.

It took about 45 minutes or so and we were done.

With no warning, Greg announced that I wanted to talk to everyone for a moment. My adrenalin soared.

It took all the courage I could muster to walk to the front and turn around and address the guys.

They all sat down and were silent. You could have heard a pin drop.

Urges by Gary Hennerberg

I paused, not knowing exactly how to launch into everything I wanted to say.

"I haven't lost my mind. I didn't lose a bet. And I'm not undergoing chemotherapy," I began. There was an audible sigh of relief when I said it wasn't chemo. It hadn't occurred to me that there would be guys who would think that I had cancer.

I paused again.

"I haven't had a full head of hair since about the age of 6," I said. "As a child, I had, and still have, a compulsive disorder. Some say it's a body focused repetitive behavior. I pull my hair.

"It's something I'm unable to stop doing and I have little control over, just as some people have no control over eating, drinking, gambling, and other urges.

"It has a name. It's called trichotillomania. I don't like the name, but that's what it is.

"For years I've worn a hair replacement. It was the only way I could see myself as I should have looked.

"But for the past year or so I've gone through a transformation of sorts. Working with a trainer and having lost weight I realized how much the hair replacement was holding me back from physical activity.

"So I decided it was time to stop wearing the hair replacement and shave my head. And I've decided that I'm not going to keep this a secret any longer."

23 — Turning Point

I realized that I had said about all I was going to say when my words trailed off and I repeated:

"It's just not going to be a secret anymore...."

At that moment, the guys started to applaud, and one-by-one they all stood up. The applause kept coming and coming, getting louder and louder. They cheered me.

I was stunned. I stood in front of about a hundred guys paralyzed, not at all expecting that response. In a moment I returned to my assigned place on the risers so we could continue. As I walked back to my spot, Jim commented to everyone about the radiant expression on my face while singing that night. It was obvious to him that I was very happy with what I had done.

After rehearsal, countless guys walked up to me to tell me how hard that had to have been for me. That I was brave. One guy told me he had a brother who pulled his hair. A teacher told me he had a student in his class who was a hair puller. A counselor told me he had counseled kids who pulled their hair. I realized that

> I realized that trich may be observed by more people than I had ever realized.

Urges by Gary Hennerberg

trich may be observed by more people than I had ever realized. The outpouring of support was amazing.

I slowly walked to my vehicle for the drive home. I unlocked my truck and got in, hoping the interior lights would dim quickly. I didn't want anyone to see me crying.

And there, alone in my truck in a dark parking lot, I sat for several minutes with tears pouring down my face because of what had happened.

That evening was a turning point in my life. I had been accepted. The guys cheered for me. And I could move on with my life without the cloud of trichotillomania hanging over me. From this point forward, hair pulling would be relegated to merely an asterisk in my life.

Chapter 24
Afterword

After this shell of my body has died, I believe my spirit will go on. I'm convinced my body won't go with me. For when I arrive at that place — call it heaven or another space — my spirit will arrive without my body.

My spirit will be released from all human conditions. I won't arrive as a hair puller. Or as an extra tall human being. I won't arrive with the human issues, urges, compulsions, and personality possessed inside a physical body.

I'll be free.

And I expect God will ask me how I did on earth with the complex weave of fabric that defined that body, that person that I am now.

God will want to know how I accepted myself. God will want to know what I did with the talents, strengths, and issues in my life. Did I wallow in self-pity? Did I hold up my head, chin forward, and march on with the hand I was dealt? Did I use my issue — trichotillomania — to somehow make the world a better place? A more accepting place?

The opening of my heart and soul in these chapters may be one way for me to have accomplished a mission on earth. But for you, the journey may be more about self-acceptance.

Urges by Gary Hennerberg

Or finding a talent that is part of your composition and then using it for great things. Or one of certainly hundreds or thousands of ways to use whatever you were given, to accept it, and to carry on.

I've determined that my prayers were indeed answered, just not in the way I had expected. I had wanted God to rid me of this mysterious urge to pull my hair. But trichotillomania is part of my physical make-up. My DNA. My fabric. Rather, God answered my prayers by giving me a life with talents that were molded by having trichotillomania.

> I've determined that my prayers were indeed answered, just not in the way I had expected.

I can't imagine who I would have become instead. I am fortunate to have had parents that love me unconditionally. A wife who has become a soul mate who will forever be part of my human existence. Daughters I treasure and adore. And a life that I'm proud to have lived. There's nothing more that I could have asked for to have made my life better. Without trichotillomania, I would have become a different human being.

CHAPTER 25
Prayer

Dear Lord,

I ask that you hear this prayer.

That you will teach me to accept the way that you have created me.

Free me to live a life on this earth where I may be a blessing to others.

Serve as a role model for those in need.

Share love where it's needed.

Understand that under the façade of skin and flesh of every human being is someone who may, deep down, be hiding an issue or an urge.

May we all show compassion and understanding.

Give support. Serve people in need.

And be an inspiration to humankind.

Hear a new approach to comfort, hope, and encouragement

From *Urges* author Gary Hennerberg

Now you can listen to Gary's comforting words on CD with his audio program named *Doses of Comfort for Hair Pullers*.

Gary will take you on a mesmerizing journey as he suggests ways for you to manage many of the emotional issues experienced by hair pullers.

He will give you strategies toward self-acceptance, how to overcome shame, how to give and receive unconditional love, become assertive, build your self-esteem, set yourself up for successful thinking, discover your gifts and talents, and how to be at ease around people. Listen to this CD at home, in your car, or download it to your iPod and listen anywhere.

For more information,
and to order your copy now, go to

www.Manage-Trich-Urges.com